PUBLISHER'S NOTE

Ancient Chinese classic poems are exquisite works of art. As far as 2,000 years ago, Chinese poets composed the beautiful work *Book of Poetry* and *Elegies of the South*. Later, they created more splendid Tang poetry and Song lyrics. Such classic works as *Thus Spoke the Master* and *Laws Divine and Human* were extremely significant in building and shaping the culture of the Chinese nation. These works are both a cultural bond linking the thoughts and affections of Chinese people and an important bridge for Chinese culture and the world.

Mr. Xu Yuanchong has been engaged in translation for 70 years. He won the Lifetime Achievement Award in Translation conferred by the Translators Association of China (TAC) in 2010, and won the "Aurora Borealis" Prize for Outstanding Translation of Fiction Literature, conferred by the Federation of International Translators (FIT) in 2014. He is honored as the only expert who translates Chinese poems into both English and French. After his excellent interpretation, many Chinese classic poems have been further refined into perfect English and French rhymes. This collection of Classical Chinese Poetry and Prose gathers his most representative English translations. It includes the classic works *Thus Spoke the Master, Laws Divine and Human* and dramas such as *Romance of the Western Bower, Dream in Peony Pavilion, Love in Long-life Hall* and *Peach Blooms Painted with Blood*. The largest part of the collection includes the translation of selected poems from different dynasties. The selection includes various types of poetry. The selected works start from the pre-Qin era to the Qing Dynasty, covering almost the entire history of classic poems in China. Reading these works is like tasting "living water from the source" of Chinese culture.

We hope this collection will help English readers "understand, enjoy and delight in" Chinese classic poems, share the intelligence of Confucius and Lao Tzu (the Older Master), share the gracefulness of Tang poems, Song lyrics and classic operas and songs and promote exchanges between Eastern and Western culture. We also sincerely invite precious suggestions from our readers.

出版前言

中国古代经典诗文是中国传统文化的奇葩。早在两千多年以前，中国诗人就写出了美丽的《诗经》和《楚辞》；以后，他们又创造了更加灿烂的唐诗和宋词。《论语》《老子》这样的经典著作，则在塑造、构成中华民族文化精神方面具有极其重要的意义。这些作品既是联接所有中国人思想、情感的文化纽带，也是中国文化走向世界的重要桥梁。

许渊冲先生从事翻译工作70年，2010年荣获"中国翻译文化终身成就奖"，2014年荣获国际译联颁发的"北极光"杰出文学翻译奖。他被称为将中国诗词译成英法韵文的唯一专家，经他的妙手，许多中国经典诗文被译成出色的英文和法文韵语。这套"许译中国经典诗文集"荟萃许先生最具代表性的英文译作，既包括《论语》《老子》这样的经典著作，又包括《西厢记》《牡丹亭》《长生殿》《桃花扇》等戏曲剧本，数量最多的则是历代诗歌选集。这些诗歌选集包括诗、词、散曲等多种体裁，所选作品上起先秦，下至清代，几乎涵盖了中国古典诗歌的整个历史。阅读和了解这些作品，即可尽览中国文化的"源头活水"。

我们希望这套许氏译本能使英语读者对中国经典诗文也"知之，好之，乐之"，能够分享孔子、老子的智慧，分享唐诗、宋词、中国古典戏曲的优美，并以此促进东西文化的交流。也敬请读者朋友提出宝贵意见。

PROJECT FOR TRANSLATION AND PUBLICATION
OF CHINESE CULTURAL WORKS
中国文化著作翻译出版工程项目

CLASSICAL CHINESE POETRY AND PROSE

300 SONG LYRICS

TRANSLATED BY XU YUANCHONG

许译中国经典诗文集

宋词三百首 | 许渊冲 译

五洲传播出版社
China Intercontinental Press

中 华 书 局
Zhonghua Book Company

CONTENTS
目　　录

27

CLASSICAL CHINESE POETRY AND PROSE

300 SONG LYRICS

TRANSLATED BY XU YUANCHONG

China Intercontinental Press   Zhonghua Book Company

PREFACE

Life is the gift of nature, but beautiful living is the gift of wisdom.

——*Greek Adage*

The ultimate good is beauty, and the ultimate joy lies in the creation or cherishing of the beautiful.

——*Schopenhauer*

If the ultimate joy lies in the creation or cherishing of the beautiful, then ancient Chinese poets may be said to have enjoyed to the full both beauty and joy in their life, for two thousand years ago they created the beautiful *Book of Songs* and *Elegies of the South*, and one thousand years ago they created the more beautiful Tang poetry and Song lyrics. Of all these the last may be said to be the most beautiful, for Song lyrics can express more refined, more delicate, more subtle feelings than Tang poetry.

The lyrics were originally songs written to a certain tune, so they may also be called tuned poetry or ci-poems. In the beginning the title of the tune and the theme of the lyric were closely related, for example, one of the earliest lyrics written to the tune of *Magpie on the Branch* reads as follows:

How can I bear to hear the chattering magpie
Announce the happy news on which I can't rely?
So thus I catch it alive when it flies to me again
And shut it in a cage where lonely't will remain.

This is the first stanza of a lyric written by an anonymous author of the Tang Dynasty(618–907), of which we find the theme and the tune title are one: the magpie on a branch. By and by many lyrics were written to this tune and their themes became less and less related to the tune title. For instance, Feng Yansi (903–960) wrote many lyrics to this tune, one stanza of which reads as follows:

> *Who says my grief has been appeased for long?*
> *Whenever comes spring,*
> *I hear it sing*
> *Its melancholy song.*
> *I'm drunk and sick before the flowers from day to day,*
> *And do not care my mirrored face is worn away.*

Here we see the lyricist describes his grief in spring which is not related with the magpie on the branch. When it came to the Song Dynasty(960–1279), the theme of the lyric might have nothing to do with the tune title, except those lyrics of which the tune was composed by the lyricist himself.

Poetry is, said Dr. Johnson, "the art of uniting pleasure with truth by calling imagination to the help of reason." How to unite pleasure with truth? As the Song Empire was the most prosperous and civilized country in the world one thousand years ago, we may find a truthful picture of the Song people's enjoyment in the following stanza written by Yan Jidao (1030–1106):

> *Time and again with rainbow sleeves you tried to fill*
> *My cup with wine that, drunk, I kept on drinking still.*
> *You danced and danced till the moon bung low over willow trees;*
> *You sang and sang till' mid peach blossoms blushed the breeze.*

Here we see how a Song poet found enjoyment in wine, woman and song.

How to call "imagination to the help of reason"? We may read the following couplet by Xin Qiji (1140–1207):

> *One night's east wind adorns a thousand trees with flowers*
> *And blows down stars in showers.*

This is a description of the Lantern Festival, the 15th day of the first lunar month, in which the lanterns are compared to flowers blown open by the east wind or to stars blown down in showers to vie in brightness with the full moon. Here we see how imagination is called "to the help of reason."

On the other hand, reason may also be called to the help of imagination. For example, Premier Yan Shu(991–1055) wrote the following stanza while imagining how sad his far-off friend was:

With hills in sight, I miss the far away in vain.
How can I bear the fallen blooms in wind and rain!
Why not enjoy the fleeting pleasure now again?

Here we see the poet tried to keep his emotions under the control of reason by persuading himself to enjoy the present pleasures instead of grieving over the fallen flowers and his friend.

Another poet who appealed to reason was Ouyang Xiu(1007–1072), who even refused to be depressed by sorrow. For instance, he wrote the following stanza to a songstress before parting with her:

Don't set to a new tune the parting song!
The old has tied our hearts in knots for long.
Until we've seen all flowers on the trees,
It's hard to bid goodbye to vernal breeze.

In other words, if we have seen all flowers on the trees, then it would not be so hard to part from spring. Here we see Ouyang knew how to seek emotional satisfaction in lyrics. Perhaps that is the reason why he could enjoy the beauty of West Lake even when

All flowers passed away, West Lake is quiet,
The fallen blooms run riot.
Catkins from willow trees

Beyond the railings fly all day like mist in breeze.

Since the lyrics were originally composed for beautiful songstresses to sing in wine shop or at farewell banquet, their theme was oftener parting and sorrow than meeting and joy. Liu Yong(987–1053) was a lyricist good at describing the parting and sorrow of lovers. In his lyrics, said Feng Xu, he is capable of complementing the complicated with the straightforward, the dense with the sparse, and the swift with the becalmed. He is able to describe what is difficult to describe and express what is difficult to express and make everything appear natural. For example, he is wellknown for the following verse:

Where shall I be found at daybreak
From wine awake?
Moored by a riverbank planted with willow trees
Beneath the waning moon and in the morning breeze.

Unlike Yan and Ouyang, he did not call reason to the help of imagination, but merged his imagination with the natural setting. His verse is, to quote Wordsworth, "the spontaneous overflow of powerful feelings recollected in tranquillity." For another example,

I shall miss you for the rest of my years,
Which can't compensate you for all your tears.

As Liu Yong was good at expressing the parting sorrow of lovers, so was Fan Zhongyan (989–1052) in describing that of soldiers on the frontier, as seen in the following verse:

(1) At the flutes' doleful sound
Over frost-covered ground
None fall asleep;
The general's hair turns white and the soldiers weep.
(2) Don't lean on rails when the bright moon appears,

Wine in sad bowels would turn into nostalgic tears.

In the first example the soldiers' feeling was aroused by the objective circumstances (flute and frost). In the second, we find Fan's imagination as vivid as Liu's. But Liu belonged to the school of "lyricism" or "delicate restraint" and Fan to that of "heroism" or the "powerful and free" school. Fan, Yan and Ouyang were good at writing short lyrics, restricted in form and in content. It was Liu Yong who began to compose long lyrics or slow tunes whose length ranges from 70 to 240 characters.

If the development of the lyric in form may be attributed to Liu Yong, then its growth in content must be credited to Su Shi (1037–1101). Su creates the lyric in the mode of Tang poetry and in so doing, he broadens its scope and elevates its status. His style is exuberant and spontaneous, characterized by his viril quality and unrestrained nature. His philosophy represents a combination of Confucianism and Taoism. "To serve the Crown" and "to attain great renown" is his Confucian ideal and "to retire as times require" and to be detached from personal gain and loss, his Taoist ideal. When Liu Yong combined the sublime with the graceful, he merged in the grand scenery, but still he could not forget his gain or loss, nor could he leave behind the description of feminine charm and amorous feeling. But in Su Shi's wellknown *Red Cliff*, which may be said, in Shelley's words, to be a "record of the best and happiest moments of the happiest and best minds," we find the following verse:

The endless river eastward flows,
With its huge waves are gone all those
Gallant heroes of bygone years;...
Life is but a passing dream.
O Moon, I drink to you who saw them on the stream.

Su merged not only in the moonlit and wave-washed scenery but also in the history of great heroes so that he became careless about gain and loss alike. Such unworldly aspiration and upright personality in him, like wind in the sky and rain on the sea, could nowhere be seen in Liu's lyric. His images of natural settings appear to be larger in scale and more expressive in function than Liu's typical elaboration of descriptive details. Even in his description of feminine charm, Liu lacks the kind of penetration and imaginative power to produce such lines as the following:

The beauty comes to drink to the flower fair;
To see her withered too she cannot bear.
Then tears and flowers
Would fall in showers.

That is perhaps the reason why Su is considered as the greatest poet of the Northern Song Dynasty.

If Su is the greatest poet, then Qin Guan (1049–1100), one of his followers, may be said to be the purest lyricist. Qin neither deals with ideal nor aspiration in his verse but describes the most subtle and delicate feeling in tangible words. For instance,

The carefree flowers fly at ease as light as dreams;
Fine threads of boundless rain drizzle like tearful sorrow.
The curtain idly bangs there, waiting for the morrow.

He has created with delicate imagery a unique world embodying his intimate personal experience. Emotion and setting in perfect fusion enhance each other like pearl and jade in a necklace. For another example,

Their tender love flows like a stream;
This happy date seems but a dream.
If love between both sides can last for aye,

Why need they stay together night and day?
This verse may be said, in Coleridge's words, to be "the best words in the best order."

Zhou Bangyan (1056–1121) has summed up the lyrical achievement of the Northern Song. Follower of Liu Yong, he inherits the form from the master while at the same time surpassing him in aspiration. In his lyrics, personal emotions are felt by various objects; that is to say, the images of seemingly independent objects are in fact the symbolic extension of his private feeling. For example, he writes about the willow:

How many times has the ancient Dyke seen
The lovers part while wafting willow down
And drooping twigs caress the stream along the town!

In fact, the ancient Dyke, wafting willow down, drooping willow twigs, all share the poet's parting grief. Thus, his "musical thought," to use Carlyle's words, has opened up a new era for such important Southern Song lyricists as Jiang Kui and Wu Wenying. It was not until his appearance that the Northern Song lyric flourished and reached its apex.

Li Qingzhao (1084–1151), who lived in the intervening period between Northern and Southern Song, was the most remarkable poetess of the Song Dynasty, Her lyrics recollect nostalgically her happy life in the North and reveal her distress in the South. "Her attempt was to establish life in words: poetry was for her a stay against time, a surety to blot out oblivion. She tried to capture the past" (*Sunflower Splendor*) or in the words of Browning, to include "the finite into the infinite." Thus her grief over her deceased husband becomes the eternal grief of a widow. This may be illustrated by the following verse:

Sitting alone at the window, how
Could I but quicken

The pace of darkness that won't thicken?
On broad plane leaves a fine rain drizzles
As twilight grizzles.
O what can I do with a grief
Beyond belief!

In 1125 the Song empire was forced by Jurchen invaders to move its capital from the North to the South, and that was the beginning of the Southern Song Dynasty. Many patriots spoke out against the humiliation and called for military action to recover the lost land, so the Southern Song verse was marked by a patriotic fervor, of which General Yue Fei's *River All Red* was typical.

Lu You (1125–1210) was the bestknown patriotic poet of the Southern Song. His poetry rises above narrow concerns and reveals an independent mind. Patriotic sentiments permeate a significant part of his verse. For instance, his everlasting regret is revealed in the following verse:

The foe not beaten back,
My hair no longer black,
My tears have flowed in vain,
Who could have thought that in this life I would remain
With a mountain-high aim
But an old mortal frame!

His failure to fulfil his high aim may be said to be, in Arnold's words, "a criticism of life."

Xin Qiji (1140–1207) was the most important lyric poet of the Southern Song Dynasty. Successor to Su Shi, he took the content over from him while at the same time putting a tighter rein on prosody than his master. But, unlike Su who had, under the influence of Taoism, a spirit of detachment when he was in exile, Xin could not, even when he lived in retirement, detach himself from his patriotism, which is revealed even in such a lyric as the lament of the departing spring:

How much more can Spring endure of wind and rain?
Too hastily it will laeve again....
But I've not heard
Spring say a word.
Only the busy spider weaves
Web all the day by painted eaves
To keep the willow down from taking leave.

Poetry is, says Robert Frost, "saying one thing and meaning another." Here when the poet says "Spring," he means the precarious Song Dynasty, the wind and rain symbolize the corruption within and the aggression from without, and the busy spider is an image of the poet himself, who tried in vain to keep the empire from its downfall. So it is said that with his appearance the lyric of the Song Dynasty flourished and reached its apex, and he is regarded as the most important lyricist of the "powerful and free" school.

On the other hand, Jiang Kui (1155–1221) was considered as the most important lyric poet of the school of "delicate restraint" of the Southern Song. Successor to Zhou Bangyan, he had some common features with his predecessor, such as painstaking choice of words and phrases, great attention paid to music and description of subtle feelings. But even in his finely chiseled verse we can find patriotic sentiment of Southern Song poetry. For example, he wrote the following verse after he visited Yangzhou overrun by Jurchen invaders:

It's now overgrown with wild green wheat and weeds.
Since Northern shore was overrun by Jurchen steeds,

Even the tall trees beside the pond have been war-torn.
As dusk is drawing near,
Cold blows the horn;
The empty town looks drear.

Overgrown weeds, overrun shores, war-torn trees, cold horns, empty towns, all reveal the deep grief of a patriotic mind, in which we see, to use the words of Yeats, "blood, imagination, intellect running together."

Wu Wenying (1200–1260) was one of the last remarkable Southern Song lyric poets. In him we see the lyrical achievements of the Northern and Southern Song combined. He is as delicate and restrained as Zhou Bangyan and as powerful and moving as Xin Qiji. Read the following verse:

Where willow branches hang like thread,
Each inch revealing
Our tender feeling.

Will you not find it as beautiful as Zhou's willow? Read another verse of his:

O willow twigs, long as you are,
Why don't you gird her waist and bar
Her way from going afar?

Will the willow twigs not remind you of Xin's busy spider trying in vain to retain the departing Spring? Besides, in his lyrics we find transcendence of time and space, which foretold the advent of modernism six hundred years ago. In short, we find in him not only lyricism and patriotism combined, but also the prototypes of symbolism and modernism. For instance,

The willowdown falls silently and Spring sheds tear;
The floating clouds cast shadows when the moon feels shy.
The east wind blows at night colder than autumn high.

How to translate such beautiful lyrics into English? I think a translated lyric should not only be faithful to the original but also as beautiful as it is in sense, in sound and in form. For example, we may read the following version of Jiang Jie's lyric written while boating on the river after the downfall of the Southern Song Dynasty:

My spring sorrow awaits wine to alley.
On the river a boat is rowing,
At the winehouse the flag is beaconing.
By the Qiuniang Ferry and on the Tainiang Bridge,
Fitful winds throw in commotion fitful rains.

This version may be said to be faithful to the original. But has it conveyed its beauty, or is it as beautiful as the lyric in Chinese? I am afraid not. In line 4 we find Qiuniang and Tainiang, which are meaningless in English, but which are in Chinese the names of two beautiful songstresses. When we read the original, the Ferry would remind us of the place where the poet bade farewell to his beloved songstress, and the Bridge of the rivershore where the lovers used to take a stroll. But the English version gives us no such idea, so it fails to bring out the original beauty in sense. The original lyric is rhymed, but the translated verse is not, so it fails to bring out the original beauty in sound. The original is composed of six lines, of which two longer lines consist each of seven characters and four shorter ones each of four; but the English version is composed of five lines of irregular length, so it has not conveyed the original beauty in form. No wonder would Robert Frost say that poetry is "what gets lost in translation." Can this loss be made up? Read the version in this book:

Can boundless vernal grief be drowned in vernal wine?
My boat tossed by waves high,
Streamers of wineshop fly.

The Farewell Ferry and the Beauty's Bridge would pine:
Wind blows from hour to hour;
Rain falls shower by shower.

Even the beauty of parallelism of the last couplet and of repetition of the last words is reproduced. If this version can afford you glimpses of the beauty of Song lyrics, I would be overdelighted to have my ultimate joy shared, for it is said that joy when shared would multiply.

Xu Yuanchong
Peking University
April 18, 2003

Zheng Wenbao

Tune: Willow Branch Song

The painted ship on vernal lake has tarried long
Until half-drunk, no one will sing a farewell song.
At last the sorrow-laden ship goes on before
Through mist and rain, through wind and waves to southern shore.

Wang Yucheng

Tune: Rouged Lips
Reflection

Laden with frowning cloud and steeped in tearful rain,
The southern shores still beautiful remain.
In riverside village flanked with fishermen's fair,
A lonely wreath of slender smoke wafts in the air.

Afar a row of wild geese fly,
Weaving a letter in the sky.
What have I done in days gone by?
Gazing from the balustrade, could I weave my way
As far as they?

KOU ZHUN

TUNE: TREADING ON GRASS

Springtime is on the wane;
The oriole's song grows old,
All red flowers fallen and green mume fruit still small.
Quiet is painted hall
Despite the drizzling rain,
Half-hidden by the screen a wreath of incense cold.

Our vow deep, deep in the heart,
We're sad to be far, far apart.
I will not look into my brass mirror dust-grey.
Silent, I lean on rails, my soul pining away;
My longing like green grass
Would join the vast dim sky, alas!

PAN LANG

TUNE: FOUNTAIN OF WINE

I still remember West Lake,
Where, leaning on the rails, I gazed without a break
On fishing boats in twos and threes
And islets in clear autumn breeze.

Among flowering reeds faint flute-songs rose,
Startled white birds took flight in rows.
Since I left, I've repaired my fishing rod at leisure,
Thoughts of waves and clouds thrill me with pleasure.

TUNE: FOUNTAIN OF WINE

I still remember watching tidal bore,
The town poured out on rivershore.
It seemed the sea had emptied all its water here,
And thousands of drums were beating far and near.

At the crest of huge billows the swimmers did stand,
Yet dry remained red flags they held in hand.
Come back, I saw in dreams the tide o'erflow the river,
Awake, I feel my heart with fear still shiver.

Lin Bu

TUNE: EVERLASTING LONGING

Northern hills green,
Southern hills green,
The green hills greet your ship sailing between.
Who knows my parting sorrow keen?

Tears from your eyes,
Tears from mine eyes;
Could silken girdle strengthen our heart-to-heart ties?
O see the river rise!

LIU YONG

TUNE: JOY OF DAY AND NIGHT

In nuptial bed for the first time we met,
I thought forever we'd together get.
The short-lived joy of love, who would believe?
Soon turned to parting that would grieve.
When late spring has grown old and soon takes leave,
I see a riot of catkins and flowers
Fallen in showers.
I am afraid all the fine view
Would go with you.

To whom may I complain of my solitude?
You oft make light of promise you have made.
Had I known the ennui is so hard to elude,
I would then have you stayed.
What I can't bear to think, your gallantry apart,
Is something else in you captivating my heart.
If one day I don't think of it,
A thousand times it would make my brows knit.

TUNE: BELLS RINGING IN THE RAIN

Cicadas chill
Drearily shrill.
We stand face to face in an evening hour
Before the pavilion, after a sudden shower.
Can we care for drinking before we part?
At the city gate
We are lingering late,
But the boat is waiting for me to depart.
Hand in hand we gaze at each other's tearful eyes
And burst into sobs with words congealed on our lips.
I'll go my way
Far, far away
On miles and miles of misty waves where sail ships,
And evening clouds hang low in boundless Southern skies.

Lovers would grieve at parting as of old.
How could I stand this clear autumn day so cold!
Where shall I be found at daybreak
From wine awake?
Moored by a riverbank planted with willow trees
Beneath the waning moon and in the morning breeze.
I'll be gone for a year.
In vain would good times and fine scenes appear.
However gallant I am on my part,
To whom can I lay bare my heart?

TUNE: THE MOON IN AUTUMN NIGHT

When we two parted then,
I thought I could not see your face again,
But unexpectedly I meet you now
At leisure, before a cup of wine.
Why should you sigh and knit your brow
As if for endless grief you'd pine!

With eyes brimming with tears,
You whisper your deep regret in my ears.
How could I find
What's hidden in your mind?
Could I believe with you there's nothing wrong,
I would refrain and stay with you for long.

TUNE: PHOENIX PERCHING ON PLANE TREE

I lean alone on balcony in light, light breeze;
As far as the eye sees,
On the horizon dark parting grief grows unseen.
In fading sunlight rises smoke over grass green.
Who understands why mutely on the rails I lean?

I'd drown in wine my parting grief;
Chanting before the cup, strained mirth brings no relief.
I find my gown too large, but I will not regret;
It's worth while growing languid for my coquette.

TUNE: WANDERING WHILE YOUNG

Slow goes my steed leaving the ancient capital;
Cicadas' trills amid the willows rise and fall.
The sun sinks down beyond the birds in flight;
The dreary plain hears the autumn wind blow.
I stretch my sight:
The sky hangs low.

The clouds, once gone, leave no more traces.
Where are my old familiar faces?
Unlike those days when I was gallant and young,
I find no more pleasure in wine, woman and song.

TUNE: WANDERING WHILE YOUNG

High and low mist-veiled trees stand by the rivershore;
The scene still looks like that of dynasties of yore.
The ancient willows fade,
Their twigs oft broken by those friends who part;
They languish like the waist of palace maid.

The setting sun turns pale, autumn's grown old,
Green grass o'ergrown with parting grief sad to behold.
The farewell song has broken my heart,
But it is heard no more;
Alone I lean upon the orchid oar.

TUNE: IMPERIAL CAPITAL RECALLED

In thin quilt on small pillow when weather is cold,
I begin to feel now the parting sorrow deep.
I toss from side to side until night has grown old;
I get up and lie down, but I can't fall asleep.
The night would appear
As long as a year.

I would have gone back to see you and stay,
But I'm so far away.
Thousands of thoughts and lame excuses only
Make me feel all the more dreary and lonely.
I shall miss you for the rest of my years,
Which can't compensate you for all your tears.

Fan Zhongyan

TUNE: WATERBAG DANCE

Clouds veil emerald sky,
Leaves strewn in yellow dye.
Waves rise in autumn hue
And blend with mist cold and green in view.
Hills steeped in slanting sunlight, sky and waves seem one;
Unfeeling grass grows sweet beyond the setting sun.

A homesick heart,
When far apart,
Lost in thoughts deep,
Night by night but sweet dreams can lull me into sleep.
Don't lean alone on rails when the bright moon appears!
Wine in sad bowels would turn to nostalgic tears.

TUNE: PRIDE OF FISHERMEN

When autumn comes to the frontier, the scene looks drear;
Southbound wild geese won't stay e'en for a day.
An uproar rises with horns blowing far and near.
Walled in by peaks, smoke rises straight
At sunset over isolate town with closed gate.

I hold a cup of wine, yet home is far away;
The northwest not yet won, I can't but stay.
At the flutes' doleful sound over frost-covered ground,
None falls asleep;
The general's hair turns white and soldiers weep.

TUNE: SONG OF THE ROYAL STREET

Withered leaves fall o'er fragrant steps shower by shower;
In night so still,
The sound seems chill.
The beaded curtain rolled up shows an empty bower.
The sky is so serene,
The Silver River hangs like Heaven's screen.
From year to year, this night
In silvery moonlight,
We're thousand miles apart.

I can't get drunk for broken is my heart;
Before I drink, wine turn to tears.
I lean on my pillow by flickering lamplight,
Drowned in the grief of lonely night.
Such deep grief as appears
On the brows or the heart
Cannot be put apart.

TUNE: CALMING WIND AND WAVES

When spring is late, the silken gown
Outshines the town.
Why not go to enjoy flowers which blend
With shadows in the pool without an end?
It seems I'm lost on the Peach Blossom Way.

No wonder mountaineers would hesitate;
Rank and fame, loss or gain depend on fate.
Butterflies love to dance, orioles to sing new song;
To the happy race they belong.
Why should we cheerless stay?

ZHANG XIAN

TUNE: BUDDHIST DANCERS

Missing my lord, I lean on railings of the tower;
From year to year sweet grass turns green before my bower.
Green as the gown he wore on taking leave,
Turning his head, the wind wafted his sleeve.

His gown must be outworn and old,
How can its green color long hold?
I fear my mirrored spring, alas!
Cannot renew as bloom and grass.

TUNE: BUDDHIST DANCERS

So soon, so soon my lord left me again.
Where trots his steed on willow-shaded lane?
I go upstairs when sinks the sun.
Does he miss me the heart-broken one?

I lean on all the balustrades in vain;
How can I not of the heartless complain?
He's not so kind as the moon bright:
Where'er I go, it's e'er in sight.

TUNE: BUDDHIST DANCERS

The zither grieves o'er Lady of River Xiang's death;
Green wave on wave exhales her everlasting breath.
Fine fingers touch the thirteen strings;
Slowly her heartfelt sorrow sings.

Her rippling eyes, feast to the sight;
Slanting jade pegs, wild geese in flight.
When her heart-breaking music thrills,
Her eyebrows lower like spring hills.

TUNE: WILLOWS ON SOUTHERN SHORE

On far-flung river shore
Light dust is raised when waves in haste roll by.
There're many farewells on willowy bridge as of yore.
It is sad to see others part;
To sever from one's own would break the heart.

After sundown,
The new moon peers at western town.
Again I gaze afar in tower high,
Wishing to follow you like slender moon
From mile to mile lest you feel lone.

TUNE: SONG OF WATER CLOCK

The banquet spread in red
With silken screen in green,
Attended by maidens fair
Of fifteen or sixteen,
Alone she knows to care
For talents fine and fill my cup with wine.

With long brows green
And small mouth, she would lean
On me and whisper in my ear:
"The winding willowy way is near
The house where you'll find me.
In front there is a blossoming apricot tree."

TUNE: TELLING INNERMOST FEELING

Before flowers, beneath the moon, shortly we met
Only to part with bitter regret.
What's more, I wake from wine and dreams
To find fallen flowers and dim moonbeams.

Flowers will bloom again;
The moon will wax and wane.
Would our hearts be the same?
I'd turn the flame
Of my heart, string on string,
Into willow twigs to retain
The breeze of spring.

TUNE: SONG OF THE IMMORTAL

Wine cup in hand, I listen to Water Melody;
Awake from wine at noon, but not from melancholy.
When will spring come back now it is going away?
In the mirror, alas!
I see happy time pass.
In vain may I recall the old days gone for aye.

Night falls on poolside sand where pairs of lovebirds stay;
The moon breaks through the clouds, with shadows flowers play.
Lamplights veiled by screen on screen can't be seen.
The fickle wind still blows;
The night so silent grows.
Tomorrow fallen reds should cover the pathway.

TUNE: MAGNOLIA FLOWER

FAREWELL TO SUN GONGSU AT ANLU

When we parted, the dream of meeting's left in vain;
Outdoors but clouds of dust raised by your horse remain.
I will not listen to songs of regret till drunk.
How can I gaze afar,
O when the sun is sunk!
With whom will you enjoy the moon in breeze tonight?
The phoenix on my pipa sobs at music light.
There's nothing to compare with love under the sky;
The river's not so deep; the mountain not so high.

YAN SHU

TUNE: TREADING ON GRASS

The mist-veiled grass looks sad in hue;
Sweet flowers shiver with cold dew.
When she leans on the rails, her heart often bewails.
The courtyard is quiet though advanced is the day;
Now and again a pair of swallows fly away.

Her girdle is too loose her silken dress to tie;
The incense burned up inch by inch will die.
The long long road would vie in length with the wide sky.
The willow branch could bar the vernal breeze from blowing.
Could it ever detain her beloved one from going?

TUNE: TREADING ON GRASS

The farewell song is sung for you;
We drink our cups and bid adieu.
I look back though fragrant dust keeps you out of view.
My horse going home neighs along the forest wide,
Your sailing boat will go farther with rising tide.

My heart broken in painted bower,
My eyes worn out in lofty tower,
The sun sheds departing rays on the parting one.
Boundless and endless will my sorrow ever run;
On earth or in the sky it will never be done.

TUNE: SILK-WASHING STREAM

A song filled with new words, a cup filled with old wine,
The bower is last year's, the weather is as fine.
Will last year reappear as the sun on decline?

Deeply I sigh for the fallen flowers in vain;
Vaguely I seem to know the swallows come again.
In fragrant garden path alone I still remain.

TUNE: SILK-WASHING STREAM

By double-curtained bower I see swallows pass;
Red petals of late flowers fall on courtyard grass,
The winding rails' shadow mingles with ripples cold.

A sudden gale blows and ruffles emerald screen.
How many times has rain dripped on lotus leaves green?
Awake from wine, the grief to see guests gone makes me old.

TUNE: SILK-WASHING STREAM

What can a short-lived man do with the fleeting year
And soul-consuming separations from his dear?
Refuse no banquet when fair singing girls appear!

With hills and rills in sight, I miss the far-off in vain.
How can I bear the fallen blooms in wind and rain!
Why not enjoy the fleeting pleasure now again?

TUNE: BUTTERFLIES IN LOVE WITH FLOWERS

Orchids shed tears with doleful asters in mist grey;
Silk curtains chill, a pair of swallows fly away.
The moon, knowing not parting grief, sheds slanting light
Through crimson windows all the night.

Last night the western breeze blew withered leaves off trees.
I mount the tower high and strain my longing eye.
I'll send a message to my dear,
But endless ranges and streams sever us far and near.

TUNE: PURE SERENE MUSIC

On rosy paper a hand fair
Has laid the innermost heart bare.
Nor fish below nor swan above
Would bear this melancholy message of love.

At sunset on west tower alone she stands still;
The curtain hook can't hang up distant hill.
Who knows where her beloved is gone?
Green waves still eastward roll on.

TUNE: TELLING INNERMOST FEELING

Chrysanthemums and lotus blooms in fragrance vie;
The Mountain-Climbing Day is near.
The far-off village seems painted in autumn dye;
Red-leafed trees interwoven with sparse gold appear.

Water runs pale and light;
Vast are the azure skies.
The long road lost to sight,
Leaning on railings high, I strain my eyes.
Hearing wild geese's song,
How much for you I long!

TUNE: DRIPPING GOLD

Mume blossoms leak out the color of spring;
Long willow branch hangs like a string;
Green grass grows fine.
My forehead sprinkled with hoar frost,
How can I not regret golden hours lost!

In fragrant hall I entertain my guest with wine
In farewell feast.
Can I retain you for a while?
Though severed by many a mile,
There's one who would remember you at least.

TUNE: SPRING IN JADE PAVILION
SPRING GRIEF

Farewell Pavilion green with grass and willow trees!
How could my gallant young lord have left me with ease!
I'm woke by midnight bell from dun dream in my bower;
Parting grief won't part with flowers falling in shower.

My beloved feels not the grief my loving heart sheds;
Each string as woven with thousnads of painful threads.
However far and wide the sky and earth may be,
They can't measure the lovesickness o'erwhelming me.

ZHANG BIAN

TUNE: SWALLOWS LEAVING PAVILION

So picturesque the land by riverside,
In autumn tints the scenery is purified.
Without a break green waves merge into azure sky,
The sunbeams after rain take chilly dye.
Bamboo fence dimly seen amid the reeds
And thatch-roofed cottages overgrown with weeds.

Among white clouds are lost white sails,
And where smoke coils up slow,
There wineshop streamers hang low.
How many of the fisherman's and woodman's tales
Are told about the Six Dynasties' fall and rise!
Saddened, I lean upon the tower's rails,
Mutely the sun turns cold and sinks in western skies.

SONG QI

TUNE: SPRING IN JADE PAVILION

The scenery is getting fine east of the town;
The rippling water greets boats rowing up and down.
Beyond green willows morning chill is growing mild;
On pink apricot branches spring is running wild.

In our floating life scarce are pleasures we seek after.
How can we value gold above a hearty laughter?
I raise wine cup to ask the slanting sun to stay
And leave among the flowers its departing ray.

Ouyang Xiu

TUNE: EVERLASTING LONGING

A creek full of duckweed
Girt with green willow trees,
On western shore I bade my parting friend goodbye.
When I came back, the moon hung low over the hill.

On mist-veiled-rill
Blows chilly breeze.
Leaning on painted gate
Again I wait
For my friend's neighing steed;
I see gulls fly
Pair by pair
In cold air.

TUNE: TELLING INNERMOST FEELING

A light frost falls at dawn when she rolls up the screen;
She breathes to warm her hands and pencils her brows green.
Nursing the parting sorrow still,
She draws her brows long as a distant hill.

As she recalls the past,
She regrets time flies fast;
Her heart would ache.
Before she sings, she pauses awhile,
And knits her brows when she would smile.
O whose heart would not break!

TUNE: TREADING ON GRASS

Mume flowers fade before the inn,
By riverside sway willows green.
On fragrant grass in the warm air a rider's seen.
The farther he goes, the longer his parting grief grows,
Endless as vernal river flows.

Heart broken by and by,
With tearful longing eye,
His wife won't lean on railings of the tower high.
Beyond the far-flung plain mountains shut out her view;
The rider's farther away than the mountains blue.

TUNE: SONG OF HAWTHORN

Last year on lunar festive night,
Lanterns 'mid blooms shone as daylight.
The moon rose atop willow tree;
My lover had a tryst with me.

This year on lunar festive night,
Moon and lanterns still shine as bright.
But where's my lover of last year?
My sleeves are wet with tear on tear.

TUNE: DREAMING OF THE SOUTH

Southern butterflies fleet
In slanting sun go pair by pair in flight,
With body powdered white
And heart fond of stealing fragrance sweet,
Born frivolous and light.

After light rain,
With thin wings dyed in misty stain,
Just come to small courtyard with roving bees,
They fly with willowdown o'er the wall in the breeze,
Busy for flowers now and again.

TUNE: DREAMING OF THE SOUTH

See Southern willow trees
To tender flowers smile with ease!
The fallen petals will adorn your cup of wine;
The willow branches hanging low caress your head,
Each inch a beauty spread.

See the Southern moon look
Now like a mirror, now like a hook:
A mirror in which no rosy faces shine,
A hook on which hangs no curtain red,
It ever shines on sleepless bed.

TUNE: SPRING IN JADE PAVILION

In front of wine I'll tell you of my parting day;
Your vernal face dissolves in tears before I say.
Lovers are born with sentimental feeling heart;
Nor moon nor wind has taken in their grief a part.

Don't set to a new tune the parting song!
The old has tied our hearts in knots for long.
Until we have seen all flowers on the trees,
It's hard to bid goodbye to vernal breeze.

TUNE: SPRING IN JADE PAVILION

Since your departure, I know not how far you've gone.

With tearful eyes, how sad and dreary to be alone!

The farther you go away, the fewer your word;

No letter-bearing fish in water wide is heard.

At dead of night the bamboos beat Autumn's refrain;

Leaf on leaf, sound on sound cry out my grief and pain.

I seek for you on dreaming pillow with deep sighs,

But no dream comes to me, the lamp flickers and dies.

TUNE: A SOUTHERN SONG

Her golden-ribboned hair

With jeweled comb so fair,

She comes before the window to ask me with a smile:

"Are my eyebrows penciled in fashionable style?"

Leaning on me so long that I can't write a line,

She wastes her time without tracing any design,

Only asking me how to spell these words:

"A pair of love-birds."

TUNE: RIVERSIDE DAFFODILS

The thunder faints away beyond the willows green;
The raindrops drip from lotus leaves after the shower.
A quivering rainbow is seen,
Shut out of view by Western Tower.
We lean on rails alone
To watch the rising moon.

A pair of swallows fly back to the painted eave;
Through fallen curtain they peep and perceive
The wavy mat still spread cold on the bed
As if none had slept in,
But by the crystal pillows twin
There is left a hairpin.

TUNE: COMPLAINT OF A GALLANT

I pine for him all day.
Who knows my misery and anxiety
Gnawing without my knowledge at my heart?
Quiet awhile, but suddenly
I know not where to settle down or live apart.

Inch by inch my heart is broken away.
What can I say?
How much it grieves!
O how can I refrain
From talking about him now and again!
In vain I wipe away my lovesick tears with sleeves.

TUNE: BUTTERFLIES IN LOVE WITH FLOWERS

Deep, deep the courtyard where he is, so deep
It's veiled by smokelike willows heap on heap,
By curtain on curtain and screen on screen.
Leaving his saddle and bridle, there he has been
Merry-making. From my tower his trace can't be seen.

The third moon now, the wind and rain are raging late;
At dusk I bar the gate,
But I can't bar in spring.
My tearful eyes ask flowers, but they fail to bring
An answer, I see red blooms fly over the swing.

SIMA GUANG

TUNE: THE MOON OVER THE WEST RIVER

Loosely she has done up her hair;
Thinly she has powdered her face.
In rosy smoke and purple mist she looks so fair;
As light as willowdown she walks with grace.

Before we part, we long to meet;
Amorous, she seems not in love.
Awake from wine and songs so sweet,
The courtyard is still and bright the moon above.

Wang Anshi

TUNE: FRAGRANCE OF LAUREL BRANCH
IN MEMORY OF THE ANCIENT CAPITAL

I climb the height
And stretch my sight:
Late autumn just begins its gloomy time.
The ancient capital looks sublime.
The limpid river, beltlike, flows a thousand miles;
Emerald peaks on peaks tower in piles.
In the declining sun sails come and go;
Against west wind wineshop streamers flutter high and low.
The painted boat
In cloud afloat,
Like stars in Silver River egrets fly.
What a picture before the eye!

The days gone by
Saw people in opulence vie.
Alas! Shame on shame came under the walls,
In palace halls.
Leaning on rails, in vain I utter sighs
Over ancient kingdoms' fall and rise.
The running water saw the Six Dynasties pass,
But I see only chilly mist and withered grass.
Even now and again
The songstresses still sing
The song composed in vain
By a captive king.

TUNE: SILK-WASHING STREAM

Half moss-hidden is my courtyard a hundred acres wide,
Before my gate a winding path by riverside.
Who would visit one fond of leisure and free hours?

Spring in my courtyard girt with corridors is still;
Two or three peach and apricots stand near the hill.
For whom are they blooming and then fall in showers?

TUNE: SONG OF A SOUTHERN COUNTRY

The capital's been ruled by kings since days gone by.
The rich green and lush gloom breathe a majestic sigh.
Like dreams has passed the reign of four hundred long years,
Which calls forth tears.
Ancient laureates were buried like their ancient peers.

Along the river I go where I will;
Up city walls and watch towers I gaze my fill.
Do not ask what has passed without leaving a trail!
To what avail?
The endless river rolls in vain beyond the rail.

TUNE: BUDDHIST DANCERS
OLD VERSES REARRANGED

By waterside the crabapple flowers run riot;
You know what they look like on rivershore so quiet.
In cold moonlight while petals fall with ease,
Across the stream blows fragrant breeze.

Golden orioles warble on the tree nearby;
Their warbling echoes low and high.
I sit as I please on moss fine,
Stroll or float with a cup of wine.

WANG ANGUO

TUNE: PURE SERENE MUSIC

Spring cannot be retained,
Though orioles have exhausted their song.
The ground is strewn with fallen reds like brocade stained,
The southern garden washed by rain all the night long.

For the first time the songstress plucked pipa string;
At dawn her yearning soars into the sky.
The painted hall with crimson door's no place for spring;
The vernal breeze with willowdown wafts high.

TUNE: SHORTENED FORM OF MAGNOLIA FLOWER

Beneath the painted bridge water flows by;

No fallen flowers wet with rain can ever fly.

At dusk the moon is seen;

On horse I still smell the fragrance behind the screen.

Silently lingering around,

Where will my dreaming soul tonight be found?

Unlike the weeping willow,

Whose down will fly into her room and on her pillow.

YAN JIDAO

TUNE: RIVERSIDE DAFFODILS

Awake from dreams, I find the locked tower high;

Sober from wine, I see the curtain hanging low.

As last year spring grief seems to grow.

Amid the falling blooms alone stand I;

In the fine rain a pair of swallows fly.

I still remember when I first saw pretty Ping,

In silken dress embroidered with two hearts in a ring,

Revealing lovesickness by touching pipa's string.

The moon shines bright just as last year;

It did see her like a cloud disappear.

TUNE: BUTTERFLIES IN LOVE WITH FLOWERS

I dreamed of roving on the southern rivershore,
However far I might go,
I could not find the fair one I adore.
To whom could I tell of my woe?
Awake, I am as sorrow-laden as before.

I would put down my lovesickness in black and white,
No swan above nor fish below
Would bring to her the love letter I write.
I can but pluck the strings to sing my woe;
My broken heart would break the strings of zither tight.

TUNE: PARTRIDGE IN THE SKY

Time and again with rainbow sleeves you tried to fill
My cup with wine that, drunk, I kept on drinking still.
You danced till the moon hung low over the willow trees;
You sang until amid peach blossoms blushed the breeze.

Then came the time to part,
But you're deep in my heart.
How many times have I met you in dreams at night!
Now left to gaze at you in silver candlelight,
I fear it is not you,
But a sweet dream untrue.

TUNE: SONG OF HAWTHORN

She never likes to cross the river far
And moves towards its head, where lovebirds are.
She sets her orchid boat adrift at leisure
And goes astray like lovebirds seeking pleasure.

An unexpected fickle cloud unseen
Turns into drizzling rain behind the screen.
Her greenish sleeves can't stand the cold. To whom
Could she complain but to the lotus bloom?

TUNE: GATHERING MULBERRIES

Since autumn came, my soul has been consumed for you,
Your letters still so few.
At home or on the way,
Could we look at each other as in olden day?

In south tower we sat side by side, hand in hand,
Known to wind and moonbeams.
But since you left the land,
Where could we sit again side by side but in dreams?

TUNE: PURE SERENE MUSIC

I could not persuade you to stay;
Drunk, you untied the cabled boat and went away.
Dipping the oars into green waves of spring,
You'd pass all trees where golden orioles sing.

The ferry's green with willows, leaf on leaf
And twig on twig reveal the parting grief.
Write no more letter if you forget the fresh shower
Brought by the cloud for thirsting flower!

TUNE: MAGNOLIA FLOWER

The sun sets over the garden swing and curtained bower;
Within embroidered doors my pen's made verse with ease.
Red apricots fade over the wall after the shower;
Green willow catkins out of doors waft in the breeze.

Where is my morning cloud leaving nor word nor trace?
She must have gone into another's vernal dream.
My piebald horse still knows my old-time roving place;
It neighs on passing painted bridge over eastern stream.

TUNE: SPRING IN JADE PAVILION

With orioles and flowers your saddled horse may stay;
You'd better go eastwards on the southern pathway.
Let vernal thoughts run riot as cloud o'er the town;
Make light of the ways of the world as willow down!

Men are misled by glory vain since olden days.
Do not belie yourself and trust not the world ways!
I would advise you to drown your sorrow in wine;
This is a place where you need not regret nor pine.

TUNE: THE LOVER'S RETURN

Old perfume and face powder smell as before;
To my regret your love's no more.
You sent me but few lines in spring,
Still fewer words does autumn bring.

Cold phoenix quilt for two,
And lovebird pillow lonely,
My sorrow can be drowned in wine only.
E'en if I dream of you, the dream will not come true.
Now you won't come in dreams, what can I do?

TUNE: SILK-WASHING STREAM

From day to day we vie in painting eyebrows long,
As light-hearted as wafting clouds and willowdown
My heart won't wed a gallant fond of wine and song.

The wine I spilt left stains on my fan of songstress;
The flowers I played with, perfumed my dancing gown.
Shedding tears all the spring, I tell my loneliness.

TUNE: TELLING INNERMOST FEELING

I oft remember your robe when green grass is seen,
Perfumed by incense burnt your girdle green.
All is quiet along the balustrade,
On which we leaned when daylight began to fade.

The breeze is full of grace,
The moon has left no trace,
My soul is steeped in hidden grief.
And I would try
To write it on a withered flower or leaf
And send it to the morning cloud on high.

TUNE: ROUGED LIPS

When flowers herald spring again,
Why won't my lord come back with flowers as before?
Now spring begins to wane;
I've broken all his willow twigs before the door.

Heaven above
Tells us to love.
Why are we kept apart so long?
Since he sang farewell song,
Even wine grieves,
Mingled with tears, it's stained my sleeves.

TUNE: WANDERING WHILE YOUNG

The eastern water and the western part,
Oh, but at last
They'll merge into one stream.
The fickle clouds have not a heart;
Though they have passed,
At night they'll come into your dream.

But woman is more fickle than water and cloud.
Alas! but when
May I meet the fickle one again?
On thinking over, I've been overflowed
With heartbreaks.
Oh, but what difference this time makes!

TUNE: DELAYING SPRING'S DEPARTURE

By painted screen vaguely I dream
Of clouds and waves in the celestial stream.
Awake, I take rosy paper in hand
And send a letter to the fairyland.
Could I write on one leaf
My boundless vernal grief?

I've leaned on rails at random in the Farewell Tower
In face of Southern Riverside so far and wide.
The stream divides before our bower.
When shall I see the tears
We shed in bygone years?

TUNE: THINKING OF THE FAR-OFF ONE

Red leaves and yellow blooms fall, late autumn is done.
I think of my far-roving one.
Gazing on clouds blown away by the breeze
And messageless wild geese,
Where can I send him word under the sun?

My endless tears drip down by windowside
And blend with ink when they're undried.
I write down the farewell we bade;
My deep love impearled throws a shade
On rosy papers and they fade.

Wang Guan

TUNE: SONG OF DIVINATION

The rippling stream's a beaming eye;
The arched brows are mountains high.
May I ask where you're bound?
There beam the eyes with arched brows around.

Sping's just made her adieu,
And now I'll part with you.
If you overtake Spring on southern shore,
Oh, stay with her once more!

Su Shi

TUNE: LAMENT OF A FAIR LADY

Who's playing on the flute a gloomy tune,
Breaking the green window's dreary dream?
The dreary mist veils the new moon,
Outspread in the sky over the stream.

You linger still though you must go.
Flowers and willow down will fall tomorrow.
They will see your boat off, laden with sorrow,
But still the stream will eastward flow.

TUNE: DRUNK WITH SOUL LOST
LEAVING THE RIVERSIDE TOWN

The crescent moon veiled by cloud light,
I wake from wine when my boat sets sail at midnight.
Turning my head toward the mist-veiled lonely town,
I only remember the farewell song,
But not when from the wineshop I got down.

Hood wry, fan dropped, I slipped from wicker bed.
Whom can I tell the dreary dream I dread?
When from this floating life may I take rest?
My hometown in southwest,
Why do I oft in southeast bid adieu as guest?

TUNE: SONG OF A SOUTHERN COUNTRY
FAREWELL TO A FRIEND

Turning my head, I find rugged mountains bar the sky,
I can no longer see you in the town.
Who can be like the hilltop tower looking down,
So high?
It welcomed you from the west and bids you goodbye.

I come back at dusk in a gentle breeze.
On chilly pillow how can I dream with ease?
Where will the flickering lamp shed its lonely light
Tonight?
When autumn rain no longer falls drop by drop,
Oh, will tears stop?

TUNE: PRELUDE TO WATER MELODY

How long will the full moon appear?
Wine cup in hand, I ask the sky.
I do not know what time of year
It would be tonight in the palace on high.
Riding the wind, there I would fly,
Yet I'm afraid the crystalline palace would be
Too high and cold for me.
I rise and dance, with my shadow I play.
On high as on earth, would it be as gay?

The moon goes round the mansions red
Through gauze-draped windows to shed
Her light upon the sleepless bed.
Against man she should have no spite.
Why then when people part, is she oft full and bright?
Men have sorrow and joy, they meet or part again;
The moon is bright or dim and she may wax or wane.
There has been nothing perfect since the olden days,
So let us wish that man
May live long as he can!
Though miles apart, we'll share the beauty she displays.

TUNE: CHARM OF A MAIDEN SINGER

The endless river eastward flows;
With its huge waves are gone all those
Gallant heroes of bygone years.
West of the ancient fortress appears
Red Cliff where General Zhou won his early fame
When the Three Kingdoms were in flame.
Rocks tower in the air and waves beat on the shore,
Rolling up a thousand heaps of snow.
To match the land so fair, how many heroes of yore
Had made great show!

I fancy General Zhou at the height
Of his success, with a plume fan in hand,
In a silk hood, so brave and bright,
Laughing and jesting with his bride so fair,
While enemy ships were destroyed as planned
Like castles in the air.
Should their souls revisit this land,
Sentimental, his bride would laugh to say:
Younger than they, I have my hair turned grey.
Life is but like a dream.
O moon, I drink to you who have seen them on the stream.

TUNE: THE MOON OVER THE WEST RIVER

Like dreams pass world affairs untold,
How many autumns in our life are cold!
My corridor is loud with wind-blown leaves at night.
See my brows frown and hair turn white!

Of my poor wine few guests are proud;
The bright moon is oft veiled in cloud.
Who would enjoy with me the mid-autumn moon lonely?
Winecup in hand, northward I look only.

TUNE: THE MOON OVER THE WEST RIVER

Wavelet on wavelet glimmers by the shores;
Cloud on cloud dimly appears in the sky.
Unsaddled is my white-jadelike horse;
Drunk, asleep in the sweet grass I'll lie.

My horse's hoofs may break, I'm afraid,
The breeze-rippled brook paved by moonlit jade.
I tether my horse to a bough of green willow
Near the bridge where I pillow
My head on arms and sleep till cuckoo's songs awake
A spring daybreak.

TUNE: RIVERSIDE DAFFODILS
RETURNING TO LINGAO BY NIGHT

Drinking at Eastern Slope by night,
I sober, then get drunk again.
When I come back, it's near midnight,
I hear the thunder of my houseboy's snore;
I knock but none answers the door.
What can I do but, leaning on my cane,
Listen to the river's refrain?

I long regret I am not master of my own.
When can I ignore the hums of up and down?
In the still night the soft winds quiver
On ripples of the river.
From now on I would vanish with my little boat;
For the rest of my life on the sea I would float.

TUNE: CALMING WIND AND WAVES

Listen not to the rain beating against the trees.

Why don't you slowly walk and chant with ease?

Better than saddled horse I like sandals and cane,

Oh, I would fain,

In a straw cloak, spend my life in mist and rain.

Drunk, I am sobered by vernal wind shrill

And rather chill.

In front I see the slanting sun atop the hill;

Turning my head, I find the dreary beaten track.

Let me go back!

Impervious to wind, rain or shine, I'll have my will.

TUNE: WANDERING WHILE YOUNG
WRITTEN AT RUNZHOU

Last year we bade adieu
Outside the town;
Snow flew like willow down.
Like snow willow down flies,
But I can't come back to see you.

The screen uprolled, to wine I invite the moon bright;
Through the window the breeze brings in dew.
The Moon Goddess seems to care
For the swallows in pair.
She sheds her light
Into their dream
On painted beam.

TUNE: SONG OF DIVINATION
WRITTEN AT DINGHUI ABBEY IN HUANGZHOU

From a sparse plane tree hangs the waning moon,
The waterclock is still and hushed is man.
Who sees a hermit pacing up and down alone?
Is it the shadow of a swan?

Startled, he turns his head
With a grief none behold.
Looking all over, he won't perch on branches dead
But on the lonely sandbank cold.

TUNE: RIVERSIDE TOWN
A DREAM ON THE NIGHT OF THE 20TH DAY OF THE 1ST MOON 1075

For ten long years the living of the dead knows nought,
Though to my mind not brought,
Could the dead be forgot?
Her lonely grave is far, a thousand miles away.
To whom can I my grief convey?
Revived even if she be, could she still know me?
My face is worn with care,
And frosted is my hair.

Last night I dreamed of coming to my native place;
She was making up her face
Before her mirror with grace.
Each saw the other hushed,
But from our eyes tears gushed.
Can I not be heart-broken when I am awoken
From her grave clad with pines,
Where only the moon shines!

TUNE: BUTTERFLIES IN LOVE WITH FLOWERS

Red flowers fade, green apricots appear still small,
When swallows pass
Over blue water that surrounds the garden wall.
Most willow catkins have been blown away, alas!
But there is no place where grows no sweet grass.

Without the wall there is a path, within a swing.
A passer-by
Hears a fair maiden's laughter in the garden ring.
The ringing laughter fades to silence by and by;
For the enchantress the enchanted can only sigh.

TUNE: SONG OF HAWTHORN
ON PARTING

Thrice I have bidden you goodbye;
This time we're old with sorrow.
Over white hair and beard we sigh:
Southward you'll go tomorrow.

Drunk, I'm followed by the moon bright,
Blooms wet with tears as with moonbeams
Will you not come back with moonlight?
The lakeside lane will haunt you in dreams.

TUNE: SONG OF THE SUNNY PASS
THE MID-AUTUMN MOON

Evening clouds withdrawn, pure cold air floods the sky;

The River of Stars mute, a jade plate turns on high.

How oft can we enjoy a fine mid-autumn night?

Where shall we view next year a silver moon so bright?

TUNE: SONG OF FLIRTATION

Fisherman,

Fisherman,

On the river in gentle wind and rain,

In blue straw cloak, broad-brimmed hat on the head,

He comes back late at dusk with fish white and wine red.

Come late with ease,

Come late with ease,

He plays his flute, but who knows where he is?

TUNE: SHORTENED FORM OF MAGNOLIA FLOWER
THE LUTE

Leisurely and tranquil,

When all voices are hushed, the sky and earth seem still.

Before a tune is played

By fingers and lute of jade, its feeling is conveyed.

The breeze saddens the stream,

The lute exhales an unfulfilled eternal dream.

Sleepless when back, I hear

It's music lingering all night long in the ear.

TUNE: DREAMLIKE SONG
ON THE RIVERSIDE TOWER

Towers on city walls like peaks appear;

Below the walls flow rivers old and clear.

I raise my hand to greet the southern cloud on high

Only to find my friend as far apart

As the evening sky,

Broken's my heart,

Broken's my heart

To see another night

On Southern Stream a full moon bright.

LI ZHIYI

TUNE: SONG OF DIVINATION

I live upstream and you downstream.
From night to night of you I dream.
Unlike the stream you're not in view,
Though we both drink from River Blue.

When will the water no more flow?
When will my grief no longer grow?
I wish your heart would be like mine,
Then not in vain for you I pine.

TUNE: DREAM OF A FAIR MAIDEN
RHYMING WITH LI BAI'S LYRIC

The clear stream's chill,
Steeped in the frosty wind the moon atop the hill.
The moon atop the hill
Greets clouds on high
And waves goodbye.

I do not know what day's today.
Looking afar, I see not your trace far away.
You're far away,
Sails come and go,
Two towers glow.

Huang Tingjian

Tune: Calming Wind and Waves

The rain pours down for miles and miles in western land;
All the day long like boats in water houses stand.
When comes the Mountain-Climbing Day the weather's fine.
Be drunk with wine
In front of River Shu where Hell is near at hand.

Don't laugh at an old man still proud and in high glee!
Oh, let us see
How many white-haired heads are pinned with golden flower?
I'd follow ancient poets at the Racing Tower.
Let's shoot and ride!
I'd tap them on the shoulder when we're side by side.

Tune: Pure Serene Music

Where is spring gone?
To lonely place unknown.
If anybody knows which way
She goes, please call her back to stay!

Spring's left no traces on the land;
None know where but orioles who sing
A hundred tunes none understand.
Riding the wind, over rose bush they wing.

TUNE: PARTRIDGE IN THE SKY

On yellow chrysanthemums dawns the morning chill.
Do not let your wine cup go dry while you live still!
Play on your flute when slants the rain and blows the breeze
Drunk, pin a flower on your invert hat with ease!

When you keep fit, eat better meal and drink more wine!
Enjoy your fill
With dancers sweet and songstresses fine!
Golden blooms become the young and white hair the old.
Why should I care for other people's glances cold?

TUNE: TELLING INNERMOST FEELING

One after another, waves on waves onward sweep;
A straw-cloaked man fishes with rod and line.
The pretty-scaly fish in water deep
Shall be caught though in ninety fathoms nine.

They hesitate
To take the bait,
Not hooked till late.
The water's chill

On river still;
He gazes his fill
From hill to hill,
His homeward way
Paved with moon ray.

TUNE: GATHERING MULBERRIES

For miles and miles to homeless wilderness I go,
My forehead dotted with snow,
Through the Life-and-Death Pass.
Leaving my children, I'd be a savage, alas!

'Neath dark cloud o'er bamboos home-going cuckoos cry
Round Lychee Mountain high.
In thatched cot at leisure,
Who sounds the clappers, teaching young maidens with pleasure?

TUNE: GAZING EAST OF THE RIVER

The west and east are severed by misty trees,
We cannot see the eastern road as we please.
I think I can go there only in dream,
Where I may not fear to be barred by the stream.

I've written countless letters by lamplight,
And tried to find a messenger, but in vain.
E'en if I may confide them to wild geese in flight,
It will be late autumn again.

TUNE: SONG OF DIVINATION

When I want to see you, you won't appear;
When I want to approach, you won't come near.
I ask how much love from you I may get,
Afraid it is not much more than regret.

Can I keep back my tears
And refrain from spirits low?
Distress on earth knows no frontiers,
There's no distress I do not know.

QIN GUAN

TUNE: COURTYARD FULL OF FRAGRANCE

A belt of clouds girds mountains high,
And withered grass spreads to the sky.
The painted horn at the watchtower blows.
Before my boat sails up,
Let's drink a farewell cup.
How many things which I recall of bygone days,
One and all, all and one,
Are lost in mist and haze!
Above the setting sun
I see but dots of crows;
Around a lonely village water flows.

I'd call to mind the soul-consuming hours
When I took off her perfume purse unseen,
And loosened her silk girdle in her bower.
All this has merely won me in the Mansion Green
The name of a fickle lover.
Now I'm a rover,
O when can I see her again?
My tears are shed in vain;
In vain they wet my sleeves.
It grieves
My heart to find her bower out of sight,
Lost at dusk in city light.

TUNE: RIVERSIDE TOWN

West of the town the willows sway in wind of spring.
Thinking of our parting would bring
To my eyes ever-flowing tears.
I still remember to the sympathetic tree
Her hand tied my returning boat for me
By the red bridge in the green field on that day.
But now she no longer appears,
Though water still flows away.

The youthful days once gone will never come again;
My grief is endless. When
Will it come to an end then?
While willow catkins and falling flowers fly,
I mount the tower high.
Even if my tears turn into a stream in May,
Could it carry away
My grief growing each day?

TUNE: RIVERSIDE TOWN

Like northbound swan and southward-flying swallow fleet,
By chance we meet;
Sadly we greet.
We see no more dark hair and beaming face of then
But two old men.
Don't ask about the long, long years since we did part!
What wrings the heart,
Keep it apart!

Draw from this vat rice wine we made in spring,
Every drop glistening.
There's no hurry. Fill our golden cup!
Having drunk up,
Like flowers fallen on the stream we go our way.
We'll meet someday,
But who knows where? The misty waves stretch far and nigh,
Cloudy the evening sky.

TUNE: IMMORTALS AT THE MAGPIE BRIDGE

Clouds float like works of art,
Stars shoot with grief at heart.
Across the Milky Way the Cowherd meets the Maid.
When Autumn's Golden Wind embraces Dew of Jade,
All the love scenes on earth, however many, fade.

Their tender love flows like a stream;
Their happy date seems but a dream.
How can they bear a separate homeward way?
If love between both sides can last for aye,
Why need they stay together night and day?

TUNE: SHORTENED FORM OF MAGNOLIA FLOWER

Gnawed by parting grief as of old,
O who would care for me, lonely and old?
If you want to know my broken heart,
Just see the incense from golden censer part!

My eyebrows ever knit,
No vernal breeze can smooth them, not a bit.
Weary, I lean on tower high.
What do I see but grievous wild geese passing by!

TUNE: SPRING IN PAINTED HALL

Lanes paved with fallen reds, the pool's full to the brim;
In drizzling rain the sunrays swim.
The apricot garden languishes with cuckoos' cries.
What can I do when away spring flies?

I mount alone the willow-shaded tower,
Leaning on rails, my hand plays with a flower.
Silent, I let it go when sunset glows.
Who knows my grief? Who knows?

TUNE: TREADING ON GRASS
AT AN INN OF CHENZHOU

Bowers are lost in mist;
Ferry dimmed in moonlight.
Peach Blossom Land idealis beyond the sight.
Shut up in lonely inn, can I bear the cold spring?
I hear at lengthening sunset homebound cuckoos sing.

Mume blossoms sent by friends
And letters brought by post,
Nostalgic thoughts uncounted assail me oft in host.
The lonely river flows around the lonely hill,
Why should it southward flow, leaving me sad and ill?

TUNE: SILK-WASHING STREAM

In light pervading cold I mount the little tower.
What can I do with an autumn-like vernal hour?
I see on painted screen but mist-veiled running stream.

The carefree falling petals fly as light as dream;
The boundless drizzling rain resembles a tearful look.
The broidered curtain hangs idly on silver hook.

TUNE: THE LOVER'S RETURN

The cold of Southern sky dissolves into wind and rain;
The courtyard's deep in vain.
From the watchtowers wafts the young prince's song,
How the dreary night appears long!

I wake from dreams
Of native streams;
And I feel only
My soul so lonely.
After the vicissitude
I pass the New Year's Eve in solitude.
The wild geese might bring letters to a southern town,
But there're no wild geese farther down.

TUNE: BEAUTIFUL LADY YU

I see nothing but mistlike dust from tower high.
Where is the place where we bade goodbye?
At sunset out of the village there lies the bay,
Where only willow down saw your boat go away.

Branches of jadelike trees can be seen now and then.
When can I see you back again?
I would send to green mansions my secret woe.
What can I do since the river won't westwards flow?

TUNE: ROUGED LIPS

Drunk, at random I float
Along the stream my little boat.
By misfortune, among
The flowers I cannot stay long.

Misty waters outspread,
I find the slanting sun on turning my head,
And countless mountains high.
Red flowers fall in showers,
I don't remember the way I come by.

TUNE: SONG OF GOOD EVENT
WRITTEN IN A DREAM

The vernal rain hastens roadside flowers to grow;
They undulate and fill mountains with spring.
Deep, deep along the stream I go,
And hear hundreds of orioles sing.

Flying cloud in my face turns to dragon or snake,
And swiftly melts in azure sky.
Lying drunk 'neath old vines, I can't make
Out if it's north or south by and by.

MI FU

TUNE: THE MOON OVER THE WEST RIVER
AUTUMN

The lotus on the creek spreads fragrance far and nigh.
Above the green, green woods undulates hill on hill.
The autumn tints are lovely 'neath the Southern sky,
Clouds break, mist clears off, wind is still.

In silent night the icy moon will rise;
From dreams begin to wake my drunken eyes.
A lute of jade is not ashamed of its songs clear;
A new tune will be played for you to hear.

TUNE: SILK-WASHING STREAM
GAZING ON THE FIELDS

The sunrays dart on plains and streams from jade-blue sky;
Barred clouds veil hill on hill, isle on isle far and nigh;
Wild flowers by the side of the creek look still red.

I watch fish leap into the net at islet's head;
Drunk, leaning on my cane, I croon verse in the brreze;
Warm spring in early winter makes me ill at ease.

ZHAO LINGZHI

TUNE: BUTTERFLIES IN LOVE WITH FLOWERS

The wind blows willow down and cold weather away,
Fragrant pollen wafts far and near,
Red showers fall from day to day.
New wine adds to the drowse left over yesterday.
How can this spring decrease the regret of last year?

Whom to ask when gone are oriole and butterfly?
I gaze from the waterside tower high,
But no fish would bring letters here.
How annoying the autumn waves inch by inch appear!
The slanting sun only foretells night is near.

He Zhu

Tune: Partridge in the Sky

All things have changed; once more I pass the city gate.
We came together; I go back without my mate.
Bitten by hoary frost, half of the plane tree dies.
Lifelong companion lost, one lonely lovebird flies.

Grass wet with dew
Dries on the plain;
How can I leave our old abode and her grave new!
In a half-empty bed I hear the pelting rain.
Who will turn up the wick and mend my coat again?

Tune: Song of Pounding Clothes

Regularly the beetle sounds
As on the anvil stone it pounds.
After washing her warrior's dress,
With ink and tears she writes down his address.
The package goes a thousand miles to the Jade Pass,
But the warrior is stationed farther west, alas!

TUNE: SPRING GRIEF AWAKENED

How can a sentimental heart from care be free,
So full of coquetry?
Clouds waft at ease with willowdown o'er far-flung grass
To wake spring grief, alas!

At dusk before my mirror to make up I try;
My light eyebrows feel shy.
I wait alone by leaning on riverside rail
For your returning sail.

TUNE: MY SHADED BOWER

At sunset on the Street of Red Birds did we meet;
We crossed the River Qinhuai on pleasure boat fleet;
You took off willow-down from hairpin with smile sweet.

Leaving your green-lit room, I come back to my bower,
Shaded by green plane leaves and red peony flower.
O could I but embrace you with moonlight in shower!

TUNE: HEADDRESS IN BROCADE

Wellknown the trip by riverside in mountain's shade,
The poet wrote it down on paper of brocade.
After a thousand years the new outdo the old.

The mist-veiled flowers bloom along the city wall;
The boats are loud with songs and lute strings one and all.
A laural headdress is won by the racers bold.

TUNE: SONG OF A FAIR MAIDEN

MIDNIGHT SONG

The moon at midnight
Shines in mid-court on pear blossoms white.
Pear blossoms white
Can't stand the flood
Of cuckoos' tears and blood.

My lord, why should no message come from you?
The mulberries-shaded lanes have swallowed our adieu.
Swallowed our adieu,
The water seems
To sob in streams.

TUNE: SONG OF A FAIR MAIDEN

Dim morning sky,
Away along the stream hundreds of birds cry.
Away birds cry.
Gone is the one on waves alone,
Empty the bower to watch the moon.

East of the Eastern Gate this day last year,
How bright did dresses and red peach blossoms appear!
Peach blossoms red
In bloom are shed
By east wind overhead.

TUNE: GREEN JADE CUP

Never again will she tread on the lakeside lane.
I follow with my eyes
The fragrant dusts that rise.
With whom is she now spending her delightful hours,
Playing on zither string,
On a crescent-shaped bridge, in a yard full of flowers,
Or in a vermeil bower only known to spring?

At dusk the floating cloud leaves the grass-fragrant plain;
With blooming brush I write heart-broken verse again.
If you ask me how deep and wide I am lovesick,
Just see a misty plain where grass grows thick,
A townful of willow down wafting on the breeze,
Or drizzling rain yellowing all mume-trees!

TUNE: BUDDHIST DANCERS

The painted boat carries my parting grief away.
Why should a fair wind follow me all the day?
On boundless waves late sets the sun.
When will my homesickness be done?

Who'll share with me this lonely night?
In dreams I have but you in sight.
But when from my dream I awake,
Parting again makes my heart break.

TUNE: PURE SERENE MUSIC

Languid, I drank a cup of adieu,
And held you fair hand anew.
I said, pointing in the courtyard to willow-trees,
I'd come back with the first leaf blown off by west breeze.

Why should I not tether my lonely boat?
How much parting grief could I keep afloat?
The moon shines now again so bright;
We're in two towers steeped in the same moonlight.

TUNE: GATHERING MULBERRIES

Inns and pavilions are places to meet and part.
How often drunk with a sweetheart?
So sad our parting appears!
Hearing songs of adieu, can I hold back my tears?

Who pities me in lonely boat on dreary night?
Where is the fishing site?
When wine is cold and lamplight dim,
How can my heart not break, grief-laden to the brim?

ZHOU BANGYAN

TUNE: SOVEREIGN OF WINE

A row of willows shades the riverside.

Their long, long swaying twigs have dyed

The mist in green.

How many times has the ancient Dyke seen

The lovers part while wafting willowdown

And drooping twigs caress the stream along the town!

I come and climb up high

To gaze on my homeland with longing eye.

Oh, who could understand

Why should a weary traveller here stand?

Along the shady way,

From year to year, from day to day,

How many branches have been broken

To keep memories awoken?

Where are the traces of my bygone days?

Again I drink to doleful lays

In parting feast by lantern light,

When pear blossoms announce the season clear and bright.

Oh, slow down, wind speeding my boat like arrow-head;

Pole of bamboo half immersed in warm stream!

Oh, post on post

Is left behind when I turn my head.

My love is lost,
Still gazing as if lost in a dream.

How sad and drear!
The farther I'm away,
The heavier on my mind my grief will weigh.
Gradually winds the river clear;
Deserted is pier on pier.
The setting sun sheds here and there its parting ray.
I will remember long
The moonlit bower visited hand in hand with you,
And the flute's plaintive song
Heard on the bridge bespangled with dew.
Lost in the past now like a dream,
My tears fall silently in stream.

TUNE: BUDDHIST DANCERS

The Milky-Way-like river winds from bend to bend,
Cranes fly over pure green waves with which wild ducks blend.
Where is the returning boat of my dear one?
From riverside tower I see but the setting sun.

Jealous of trees with mume blossoms aglow,
Heaven covers their branches with snow.
If he uprolls the curtain in his bower,
He'd pity the cold riverside flower.

TUNE: SPRING IN JADE PAVILION

We did not live long with ease on Peach Blossom Stream;
The severed lotus root can't be united again.
I waited for you on the bridge with red railings then;
Today I seek alone, mid yellow leaves our dream.

The countless mist-veiled peaks have dyed the sky in blue;
Twilight is reddened by sunset borne by wild geese.
You're like the cloud sunk in the river by the breeze;
My heart like willow down wet with rain clings to you.

TUNE: EVERLASTING LONGING
WRITTEN IN A BOAT

In a fair breeze I float,
When stops the evening rain,
By leafy forest's shade set off my birdlike boat,
At sunset the fair leaning on rails waits in vain.

I fix my gloomy gaze
And recall my trips alone.
A leaflike boat on Griefless Lake in autumn haze,
Braved wind and waves, heading for the Town of Stone.

TUNE: CRANE SOARING INTO THE SKY
WRITTEN IN THE LONG LIFE VILLAGE

Long rain clears off when blows soft summer breeze,
Cicadas trill pellmell atop tall willow trees.
From my bower the garden pool's far away;
New lotus leaves stir when fish play.

Bed curtain thin
Lets feather fan blow in
Fresh air to chill
The mat and pillow from deep courtyard still.
My feeling as the weather nice
Brings me to earthly paradise.

TUNE: SONG OF MOUNTAIN PASS AND RIVER

Autumn's now cloudy and now fine,
Gradually on the decline.
It turns dreary and chill
In a courtyard still.
I stand to listen to cold breeze;
In thick clouds I see no wild geese.

No one is left deep in the silent night,
But lonely candle sheds on lonely walls its light.
Awake from wine and autumn song,
How can I pass this endless night so long?

CHEN GUAN

TUNE: SONG OF DIVINATION

My body is a leaflike boat,
And like the tide all events flow.
I let my boat on the rising tide float;
So on the waves I come and go.

The tide may fall and rise again;
As of old will things stop and start.
Next time when I drink alone, the moon will not wane,
But we're a thousand miles apart.

Xie Yi

TUNE: RIVERSIDE TOWN

The streamer flies among apricots in the breeze;
Brimming water wide spread,
Fallen petals dye the shore red.
A boat athwart the ferry, the willow trees
Cast shadows deep green.
I gaze southward on far-flung mountains high,
My love cannot be seen,
But grass spreads to the sky.

At sunset the mist veiled her bower,
Her rosy face sweet like a flower,
With eyebrows penciled like a hill.
I remember still
That year before the painted screen we met with smiles.
But now over the mountain pass tonight,
Severed for miles and miles,
We share only the same moonlight.

MAO PANG

TUNE: SILK-WASHING STREAM
BOATING IN EARLY SPRING WITH SNOW AND MUME BLOSSOMS NORTH AND SOUTH OF THE STREAM

Snow on cold mist-veiled northern shore looks like mume white;
Mume blooms on southern shore like piles of snow run riot:
Two terraces of jade north and south in moonlight.

Clouds are near as if I were sitting in the sky;
Mume blossoms seem to breathe in wine their spirit quiet.
How many shores see them bring spring back from on high?

TUNE: SILK-WASHING STREAM
BOATING ON MY WAY BACK

The reeds and willow trees slant slightly in the breeze,
I need no window screen lest I can't gaze my fill.
I'll carry round the sands the shadow of the hill.

The little bridge divides the views of riversides.
On flowers in the isle alights a dragonfly.
Can I forget this stream where'er I go 'neath the sky?

TUNE: SEPARATION REGRETTED

Her face criss-crossed with tears, a flower bathed in dew;
Her saddened eyebrows knit like distant peaks in view.
How can I not share her grief acute?
What can we do but gaze at each other mute?

My broken cloud won't bring showers for thirsting flowers,
Lonely in morning and in evening hours.
Tonight in mountains deep I'd ask the rising tide
To bring my yearning heart to her at the seaside.

SU XIANG

TUNE: DREAMLIKE SONG
WRITTEN IN SNOW

Peak on peak buried in mist and rain at daybreak
Suddenly turn to blossoms flying flake on flake,
And then shower by shower,
To accompany the lonely southern mume flower.
At nightfall,
At nightfall,
All cloud-veiled woods look like a pall.

TUNE: AT THE GOLDEN GATE
MY OLD ABODE

Where is the place?
Outdoors cold clouds pile up over the pool in face.
Will riverside cold mumes 'mid bamboos bloom or not?
A light rain drizzles o'er the cot.

Who has sent so much sorrow to this land?
By the wild pool at the ferry I stand.
Are cloudlike flowers I planted still there? Tell me please.
On mist-veiled isles undulate willow trees.

TUNE: BUDDHIST DANCERS
WRITTEN IN THE BOAT OF A FRIEND

Before my eyes mist-veiled trees on mist-veiled trees stand;
Evening clouds shed rain drop by drop on lotus blooms.
Gulls float along smoke-darkened sand;
In overbrimming green rushes autumn looms.

I've gone overseas
But stay by pools and woods.
My homeless grief won't cease;
The wind slants our white hoods.

TUNE: BUDDHIST DANCERS

I remember I was drunk before flowers last year,
But now with flowers fallen, languid I appear.
Wheat undulates like waves 'neath the fine sky;
I'm saddened by cuckoos' home-going cry.

Where can I find message-bearing wild geese?
On locust trees blows early summer breeze.
My home's beyond rainbow cloud's dream;
I'm grieved to see the full moon on the stream.

HUI HONG

TUNE: SILK-WASHING STREAM
INKY MUME BLOSSOMS

At dusk a boat is floating on the river wide,
Whose hermitage stands lonely by the riverside?
A branch of mume at leisure stretches o'er the wall.

The mume veiled in moonlight sends fragrance on the wing;
It longs for home, but only stays for coming spring.
The wind-stirred petals show their sorrow one and all.

Xie Kejia

TUNE: REMEMBERING THE SOVEREIGN OF YORE

The weeping willow trees caress the palace wall;

The vernal day seems long when there's none in the hall.

The swallows coming back are busy as before.

Remembering the sovereign of yore,

The waning moon would break our heart at the nightfall.

Wang Anzhong

TUNE: SONG OF DIVINATION
ON THE WAY TO MOUNT DAO

Before the inn two or three flowers

Blow face to face in morning hours.

One wet with dew and full of grace looks tender;

Another rises like smoke slender.

Who will pin the reds in your hair

To vie with spring to be more fair?

I know from far away they're sent to you in dreams.

The village's silent with setting moonbeams.

Ye Mengde

TUNE: SILK-WASHING STREAM
ON THE TOWER AFTER THE MOUNTAIN-CLIMBING DAY

After a fine rain it was growing cold last night;
Chrysanthemums hasten to yellow by fenceside.
The west wind sweeps the boundless blue sky far and wide.

Wild geese flying far, far away are lost to sight;
The sweet green grass unseen for ten years grieves my heart.
Slowly I sing and with a cup of wine I part.

TUNE: SILK-WASHING STREAM
PARTING WITH LU CHI

Lotus leaves and blooms mirrored in water sky-blue;
We drink from jade wine-bottle the fresh fountain-brew.
While making merry, can we forget bygone years?

A stranger here, I'll go back to my native hill;
Before parting with you, long, long I linger still.
O songstress fair, don't sing of meeting without tears!

TUNE: ROUGED LIPS
ON SUMMIT TOWER IN 1135

Who in the cloud-veiled tower speaks
And laughs alone over a thousand peaks?
Who would enjoy with me
The misty waves rolling for miles and miles I see?

Now old I grow,
Could I regain the lost land far below?
In vain I sigh:
Gallant while young, can I
Live as decrepit man and die?

TUNE: SONG OF DIVINATION
ENJOYING THE BREEZE IN PHOENIX PAVILION ON
THE NIGHT OF THE 5TH DAY OF THE 8TH MOON

The crescent moon hangs on tree-tips;
In dried pool hidden water drips.
On painted eaves I see now and then sparse stars fall,
Here and there a few dots of fireflies small.

I'm not much sick for native hill,
But homesickness haunts me still.
I'll write new songs for gatherers of lotus seed,
But find on boundless water mist-veiled reed.

WANG ZAO

TUNE: ROUGED LIPS

The crescent moon so fair,
The night so chill,
The stream so still,
I rise and scratch my hair,
The mumes cast slender shadows across windowsill.

The frosty sky so fine,
A cup in hand, I can't but pine.
Do you not know
After the wailing of the crow
I am more homesick than thirty for wine?

CAO ZU

TUNE: ROUGED LIPS

Clouds pierced by slanting sunlight,
Red shadows veil half my bower with windows bright.
Hills on hills in twilight,
Grieve the returning wild geese in flight.

For miles and miles stretches the wild plain;
Beyond the far-off flowers woods on woods extend.
I stand and gaze in vain.
Where is my old friend?
How I regret spring will soon end!

Xiang Hao

TUNE: DREAMLIKE SONG

Can cups of wine at an inn drink me down?
Drunk, can my two long long eyebrows not frown?
I cannot go to sleep.
What can I do when I'm awake from drinking deep?
Do you not know?
Do you not know
It is only for you that thinner I grow?

TUNE: DREAMLIKE SONG

Who'll sit before the bright window with me?
Only my shadow keeps me company.
The lamp put out, I go to bed, my shadow too
Will abandon me lonely.
What can I do?
What can I do?
There's left a dreary person only.

Moqi Yong

Tune: Lament of a Fair Lady

When spring has come to southern bower,
Snow melts away.
It heralds Festival of Flowers
And Lantern Day.
But a fine rain
Brings back the chill again.
I lean upon the rail.

Don't oft lean there! Of what avail?
What will you see beyond the misty rills
But misty hills?
Where is the blooming capital?
Evening clouds have veiled all.

TUNE: TELLING INNERMOST FEELING

FAREWELL TO SPRING

Whipping my steed, I'm glad to go home at daybreak,
Drunken with rainbow cloud and just awake.
Last night the rain did cease;
A pair of swallows dance in slanting breeze.

From hill to hill,
From rill to rill,
I gaze my fill...
Farewell to the spring day!
Sick for home far away,
To whom but willow down can I say?

TUNE: EVERLASTING LONGING
RAIN

Watch after watch
And drop by drop,
The rain falls on banana leaves without stop.
Within the window by the candlelight,
For you I'm longing all night.

I cannot seek for dreams,
Nor banish sorrow.
The rain cares not for what I dislike, it seems;
On marble steps it drips until the morrow.

TUNE: EVERLASTING LONGING
A STATION IN THE MOUNTAINS

The stations far and nigh
Show griefs new and gone by.
A halo encircles the cold moon over the bower;
Autumn seems clearer after a shower.

At dusk clouds barring the sky
Hang as low as mountains high.
Rustling autumn leaves and wild geese sing sad and drear;
But the roamer won't hear.

Chen Ke

Tune: Bean Leaves Yellow

In empty courtyard from players the swing is free;
The burned-out incense and dim lamplight sadden me.
On marble steps with flowing sleeves I stand alone
To watch the dimming moon
As in fine rain stands a lonely blooming pear-tree.

Zhu Dunru

Tune: Partridge in the Sky
Written at the West Capital

I am in charge of mountains and rivers divine,
Heaven tells me to be free to give order mine.
I have commanded rain to fall and wind to blow
And asked the cloud to stay and the moon to go.

Thousands of verses fine,
Hundreds of cups of wine,
I've only looked down upon the lords in power.
I would never go back high in my golden tower,
But drunk in the west capital with the mume flower.

TUNE: PARTRIDGE IN THE SKY

Drunk with mume blossoms, I won't go homewards.
The beauties clinging to my sleeves, ask for verse fine.
I write all in bright red on a belt of lovebirds;
They try to fill my jadeite cup with dark green wine.

I am already old,
But old things are no more.
I can't drink with flowers, my sleeves with tears are cold.
Now I would only sleep with closed door,
And let mume petals fly like snow in the sky.

TUNE: PARTRIDGE IN THE SKY

Your painted boat went eastward on the river clear.
How could I bear the parting sorrow sad and drear?
Since in west wind with tears in eyes we bade adieu,
Nine out of ten nights I dream of the station and you,

Clouds fly over water wide,
Wild geese over riverside,
Only amid sweet grass
Can I see leaving soul, alas!
Last time we came together to pick lotus leaves;
Now the lonely moon in the dreary breeze still grieves.

TUNE: MEASURES AT COURT

In my wandering life my bamboo cane will bear
Moonbeams and flowers fair.
Staying, I've no dislike or love,
Leaving, there's rainbow cloud above.

Roaming, I'll drink wine in a shop
And tea in a temple where I stop.
Like an oriole in flight,
None knows where I'll alight.

TUNE: LONELINESS

I heard it rain all night long till the break of day,
Accompanied by lamplight green.
My feelings now and then cannot be told.
Flowers unseen,
In vain I'm old.

It is a pity spring has passed away,
More cloudy than fine days gone by.
North and south of the River water blends with the sky.
May I ask where
To find grass fair?

TUNE: LONELINESS

I used to be detained by flowers fair,
By butterflies and orioles here and there.
While young, I was fond of being drunk and gay;
It was easy to let spring slip away.

Now it's again late spring on Southern shore.
Where is the rosy face of yore?
Do not compare my grief to falling flowers!
It can't be counted as petals falling in showers.

TUNE: TWELVE HOURS

Pale grass blends with clouds far and nigh,
The setting sun reddens the sky;
Red leaves cover the mountains high.
The western breeze
Strips off the trees;
The creek once more
Sobs as before.

Swallows and wild geese bring no news to me.
With whom may I enjoy chrysanthemums in glee?
What grieves most those who roam?
No winter garments come from home.

TUNE: SONG OF GOOD EVENT
SONG OF A FISHERMAN

Shaking my head,
I leave the land, now sober, now drunken dead.
Fishing in green straw cloak and hat I go,
Used to wearing frost and braving snow.

At nightfall when wind lulls, my fishing's done;
The crescent moon makes sky and water one.
I see moon light high and low, far and near;
A single swan appears only to disappear.

TUNE: SHORTENED FORM OF MAGNOLIA FLOWER

Uninvited to wine,
I spread a blanket and sit beneath a pine.
Drinking, I write verse fine,
Mume blossoms serve as attendants divine.

Drunken in happy hours,
When the bright moon flies down, I sleep beneath the flowers.
I dance — Who knows my delight?
My hood covered with blooms, my cup brimming with moonlight.

TUNE: GREEN WILLOW TIPS

I part with the fair in green and bright red,
Half awake from wine of last night,
My steed ready to start.
The bell lingers beyond the tower,
In the tent flickers candlelight,
The waning moon peeps into her bower.

The sleepless buries in the pillow her head,
Thinking of the wayfarer going north and south,
Unforgettable in her heart,
Invisible to her sight,
Unutterable in her mouth.

TUNE: SONG OF DIVINATION

A mume tree grows by creekside old;
It won't be locked in garden small.
In deep mountains so far away it fears no cold;
It seems to shun spring's call.

Who knows its lovely heart?
From friendship it will part.
It shows its beauty and fragrance alone,
Sought after by the moon.

TUNE: SONG OF DIVINATION

Wild geese on voyage southward fly;
In wind and rain one goes awry.
Tired, hungry and thirsty, with two wings hanging down,
It comes alone on the cold down.

Waterbirds are hard to get near;
Of arrows it oft stands in fear.
Where in the vast sea of clouds can it go along?
Who'd hear in haste its plaintive song?

TUNE: JOY OF MEETING

The east wind blows away all riverside mume flowers,
And orange blossoms blow.
In ancient Wu palaces, before the bowers,
Green mosses grow.

The empire's rise and fall
Make heroes all
Shed tears untold
And men grow old.
How I regret the sun sinks on the western side
And ebbs the evening tide!

TUNE: JOY OF MEETING

I lean on western railings of the city wall
Of Jinling in the fall.
Shedding its rays over miles and miles, the sun hangs low
To see the endless river flow.

The Central Plain is in a mess;
Officials scatter in distress.
When to recover our frontiers?
Ask the sad wind to blow over Yangzhou my tears!

MURONG YANQING'S WIFE

TUNE: SILK-WASHING STREAM

I recall bygone trips with hills and streams in view,
In mild spring breeze riverside grass and flowers sway.
Would orchid boats stay at Pavilion of Adieu!

It's easy for sweet dreams to go with running streams;
In vain will go my heart as sad morning clouds part.
Roamer, don't mount the tower to gaze far away!

Zhou Zizhi

TUNE: SONG OF DIVINATION
TO A FRIEND AT FAREWELL FEAST

Your boat will leave the northern shore at last.
When we meet again, it's south of the stream.
O how many autumns north and south will have passed?
How faces will have changed even in dream?

We are like clouds atop the hill.
Who will care if we part or stay?
Where like a lonely cloud can you go as you will?
I'm like a wild goose stray.

TUNE: PARTRIDGE IN THE SKY

Red flames of burned-up candle shed flickering light,
In chilly autumn air are drowned the screens in view.
The drizzle drips on plane trees at the dead of night,
Drop by drop, leaf on leaf remind me of your adieu.

We played on zither dear,
Incense from burner rose,
Singing the lovebirds' song, together we stayed close.
Tonight wind and rain rage in western bower drear,
How can I not shed tears
When none sings to my ears!

TUNE: BUDDHIST DANCERS

The wind blows freely and clouds come and go away;
At the heart of the lake Heaven makes the moon stay,
The long night grieves
My long, long sleeves.
In wind and water autumn looms.

Towards the dew smile lotus blooms.
On the dark stream
But fireflies gleam.
O fishers' flute, don't often blow!
The roamer's grieved, but you don't know.

TUNE: TREADING ON GRASS

My thoughts waft like gossemer light;
You'll go off as willow down flies.
In vain we gaze at each other with tearful eyes.
Thousands of willow twigs hang low by riverside,
But none of them can stop your orchid boat on the tide.

Past setting sun wild geese in flight,
On mist-veiled isle grass lost to sight,
It looks like a boundless ocean of grief and sorrow.
But now do not think of what I shall do tomorrow!
Alas! how can I pass this endless lonely night.

ZHAO JI

TUNE: HILLSIDE PAVILION

Petal on petal of well-cut fine silk ice-white,
Evenly touched with rouge light,
Your fashion new and overflowing charm make shy
All fragrant palace maids on high.
How easy 'tis for you to fade!
You cannot bear the cruel wind and shower's raid.
I'm sad to ask the courtyard sad and drear
How many waning springs have haunted here?

My heart is overladen with deep grief.
How could a pair of swallows give relief?
Could they know what I say?
'Neath boundless sky my ancient palace's far away.
Between us countless streams and mountains stand.
Could swallows find my native land?
Could I forget these mountains and these streams?
But I cannot go back except in dreams.
I know that dreams can never be
Believed, but now e'en dreams won't come to me!

LI QI

TUNE: A SOUTHERN SONG

Like a wreath of smoke rises autumn breeze;
Shower by shower
Fall withered leaves from the trees.
On Yueyang Tower I hear sad music plays.
For whom in the bower
The moon over the river sheds its gloomy rays?
The Cloud-Dreaming Lake lost in haze and rain;
The Dongting Lake spreads like a boundless plain
With its misty water green.
Alas! Where can I find the drowned Fairy Queen?
Only the feelingless river flows down
Around the riverside town.

TUNE: DREAMLIKE SONG

Spring water in the lake is deep;
'Mid dark bamboos there is no sandy way.
Who has the leisure to weep
Over petals fallen in heap?
I believe the east wind has gone away.
Just stay!
Just stay
To gaze
On the two mountains steep
In rain and haze.

TUNE: DREAMLIKE SONG

At early dawn no jade-white
Beauty is in sight.
Long, long I sigh
To clouds on high.
Green water brims over the rail-girt pool;
Beyond bamboos I find mume branch with ease
Sway in the breeze.
How wonderful!
How wonderful
To see the beauty steeped in moonlight
At dead of night!

Anonymous

TUNE: SONG OF THE ROYAL STREET

Hard blows the frosty breeze;
In frozen quilt I hear
Sad cackles of wild geese,
Cry on cry bringing grief on grief far and near.
The clouds are pale; the azure sky like water clear.
I don my robe and tell the geese,
"Stop for a while and listen please!

In little town south of the tower,
Beyond the third bridge, by the western riverside,
There stands a crimson-painted bower,
With pillar-like plane trees outside.
Please do not cry.
When you pass by,
Or my dear sleepless wife would sigh!"

LI QINGZHAO

TUNE: A SOUTHERN SONG

On high the Silver River veers;
On earth all curtains are drawn down.
My mat and pillow grow chilly, wet with tears,
I rise to take off my silk gown,
Wondering how old night has grown.

Small is the green lotus on the robe I caress,
And sparse the leaves embroidered in thread of gold.
In old-time weather still I wear my old-time dress,
Only my heart feels cold
And the mood I'm in is different from that of old.

TUNE: DREAMLIKE SONG

Last night the strong wind blew with a rain fine;
Sound sleep did not dispel the aftertaste of wine.
I ask the maid rolling up the screen.
"The same crab apple," says she, "can be seen."
"But don't you know,
Oh, don't you know
The red should languish and the green should grow?"

TUNE: PLAYING FLUTE RECALLED ON PHOENIX TERRACE

Incense in gold
Censer is cold;
I toss in bed,
Quilt like waves red.
Getting up idly, I won't comb my hair;
My dressing table undusted, I leave it there.
Now the sun seems to hang on the drapery's hook.
I fear the parting grief would make me sadder look.
I've much to say, yet pause as soon as I begin.
Recently I've grown thin,
Not that I'm sick with wine,
Nor that for autumn sad I pine.

Be done, be done!
Once you are gone,
However many parting songs we sing anew,
We can't keep you.
Far, far away you pass your days;
My bower here is drowned in haze.
In front there is a running brook
That could never forget my longing look.
From now on, where
I gaze all day long with a vacant stare,
A new grief would grow there.

TUNE: A TWIG OF MUME BLOSSOMS

Fragrant lotus blooms fade, autumn chills mat of jade.

My silk robe doffed, I float

Alone in orchid boat.

Who in the cloud would bring me letters in brocade?

When swans come back in flight,

My bower is steeped in moonlight.

As fallen flowers drift and water runs its way,

One longing leaves no traces

But overflows two places.

O how can such lovesickness be driven away?

From eyebrows kept apart,

Again it gnaws my heart.

TUNE: TIPSY IN FLOWERS' SHADE

Veiled in thin mist and thick cloud, how sad the long day!
Incense from golden censer melts away.
The Double Ninth comes again;
Alone I still remain
In silken bed curtain, on pillow smooth like jade.
Feeling the midnight chill invade.

At dusk I drink before chrysanthemums in bloom,
My sleeves filled with fragrance and gloom.
Say not my soul
Is not consumed. Should the west wind uproll
The curtain of my bower,
You'll see a face thinner than yellow flower.

TUNE: AMPLIFIED SONG OF GATHERING MULBERRIES
THE BANANA

Who's planted before my window the banana trees,
Whose shadows in the courtyard please?
Their shadows in the courtyard please,
For all the leaves are outspread from the heart
As if unwilling to be kept apart.

Heart-broken on my pillow, I hear midnight rain
Drizzling now and again.
Drizzling now and again,
It saddens a Northern woman who sighs.
What can she do, unused to it, but rise?

TUNE: DREAM OF A FAIR MAIDEN

Viewed from the tower high,
The plain is strewn with hills, veiled in thin mist far and nigh.
In thin mist far and nigh,
Dark crows come back to rest
In their dark nest,
I hear the horn sadden the evening sky.

Incense burned and wine drunk, only my heart still grieves
To see the west wind hasten the fall of plane leaves.
Falling plane leaves,
Again I see the autumn hue;
Again I've loneliness in view.

TUNE: SPRING IN PEACH GROVE

Sweet flowers fall to dust when winds abate,
Tired, I won't comb my hair though it is late.
Things are the same, but he's no more and all is o'er
Before I speak, how can my tears not pour!

'Tis said at Twin Creek spring is not yet gone.
In a light boat I long to float thereon.
But I'm afraid the grief-overladen boat
Upon Twin Creek can't keep afloat.

TUNE: SLOW SLOW SONG

I look for what I miss,
I know not what it is.
I feel so sad, so drear,
So lonely, without cheer.
How hard is it
To keep me fit
In this lingering cold!
Hardly warmed up
By cup on cup
Of wine so dry,
Oh, how can I
Endure the drift
Of evening wind so swift?
It breaks my heart, alas!
To see the wild geese pass
For they are my acquaintances of old.

The ground is covered with yellow flowers,
Faded and fallen in showers.
Who will pick them up now?
Sitting alone at the window, how
Could I but quicken
The pace of darkness that won't thicken?
On the plane leaves a fine rain drizzles
As twilight grizzles.
Oh, what can I do with a grief
Beyond belief!

TUNE: ROUGED LIPS

Lonely in my room,

Each heartstring is a thread of gloom.

Spring cannot be retained by love,

Flowers hastened to fall by raindrops above.

I lean from rail to rail,

To lighten my sorrow, but to no avail.

O where is he?

Sweet grass spreads as far as the sky.

It saddens me

To gaze on his returning way with longing eye.

Lü Benzhong

TUNE: GATHERING MULBERRIES

I'm grieved to find you unlike the moon at its best,
North, south, east, west.
North, south, east, west,
It would accompany me without any rest.

I am grieved to find you like the moon which would fain
Now wax, now wane.
You wax and wane.
When will you come around like the full moon again?

TUNE: SHORTENED FORM OF MAGNOLIA FLOWER

Last year this very night
We drank beneath the flowers under the moon bright.
Tonight by riverside
The moon is dim; we're in a boat that willows hide.

Where will you go, my friend?
Will you carry my parting grief to the river's end?
Next year before the flowers,
As we recall last year, we shall recall these hours.

Xiang Ziyin

Tune: The Lover's Return

ON MY WAY TO POYANG IN SNOW

North and south of the River covered deep with snow,
The Northern Stream must be cold, from afar I know.
Through thickest cloud I look for Northern Pass,
My heart is broken to find hill on hill, alas!

Heaven may grow old,
The sea may turn cold,
How can I drown this grief untold!
Messengers have been sent to the North now and then.
But when will His Majesty come back? O when?

TUNE: THE MOON OVER THE TOWER

Sweet flowers pass away.

From my homeland kept apart,

Deep grieves my heart.

Deep grieves my heart

With endless streams in view

And boundless mountain hue.

How can I bear the approaching Dragon Day!

My eyes are dried of tears and blood in vain is shed.

In vain blood's shed

To hear the cuckoos cry

Overhead

And see the morning breeze and waning moon on high.

TUNE: SONG OF HAWTHORN

You look like moonlight when you're near;
Far as mist-veiled bloom you appear.
When the moon's bright, it's the best hours
For us to drink amid flowers.

From loving blooms I can't refrain;
Under the moon I pine in vain.
I wish in moonlight we'd ever stay,
Unlike flowers flying away.

CAI SHEN

TUNE: AT THE GOLDEN GATE

Hear the creek sob and sigh!
Along the creek we are saying goodbye.
Our farewell's said while tears stream down in flood,
Your silk scarf stained with blood.

I may pretend to have an iron heart;
It would break with grief now we part.
Turning the head, you'll find hills hide my sail from sight,
In vain my painted boat is laden with moonlight.

TUNE: SONG OF DIVINATION

That night when the full moon shone bright,
Hand in hand we stood in moonlight.
Tonight again the sky is steeped in moon ray;
The night appears as fine as the day.

The moon and the wind still the same remain,
But I recall the waterside bower in vain.
Tomorrow I will ask you when at home you're due,
If you know how much I'm longing for you.

TUNE: EVERLASTING LONGING

The village maids not old,
With rosy sleeves uprolled,
Plant rice when yellow mumes begin to grow;
In pairs they come and go.

They sing their song
Or short or long.
Their songs regret true lovers should part.
Do they know love at heart?

TUNE: SONG OF WESTERN TOWER

How long before my tower on running water float
Ship on ship, boat on boat.
How can cold clouds and withered grass in view
Not sadden you!

How much regret!
How many tears!
Can you forget
I wait for years?
Don't any longer roam
But soon come home!

Ru Hui

TUNE: SONG OF DIVINATION
SEEING SPRING OFF

I want to see spring go away,
For I've no means to make her stay.
After all, she'd come back from year to year.
Why not forever stay here?

I cannot see the end of Southern sky
Nor where spring has gone by.
When the wind blows, like sorrow fall peach flowers;
Dot by dot fly red showers.

Wang Zhuo

TUNE: ROUGED LIPS
ON ASCENDING THE TOWER

Don't sigh for the parting spring day!
Try with a cup of wine to ask her to stay.
But she's silent and still,
The uprolled screen shows rain on western hill.

My sorrow-laden heart forces me to write
A poem on the height.
E'en countless mist-veiled hills
And countless mist-veiled rills
Won't let spring go away.

TUNE: EVERLASTING LONGING

You come so soon
And leave so soon.
Can I rely on short dreams and spring passed in vain?
It's hard to follow your traces again.

From hill to hill,
From rill to rill,
Like willow down and cloud wafting from east to west,
Where to send you my wishes best?

LI CHONGYUAN

TUNE: THE PRINCE RECALLED
SONG OF SPRING

Luxuriant grass reminds me of my roving mate.
In vain my heart breaks in willow-shaded tower high.
"Better go home!" How could I bear the cuckoo's cry!
The evening is growing late,
The rain beats on pear blossoms, I shut up the gate.

NIE SHENGQIONG

TUNE: PARTRIDGE IN THE SKY
FOR HER HUSBAND

I see you leave the town, jade-pale to sadden flower;
The willows look so green below the Lotus Tower.
Before a cup of wine I sing a farewell song;
At the fifth post I see you off on journey long.

I seek again
Sweet dreams in vain.
Who knows how deep is my sorrow?
My teardrops on the pillow
And raindrops on the willow
Drip within and without the window till the morrow.

LI MIXUN

TUNE: BUDDHIST DANCERS

From month to month in riverside town fire was spread.
Can I bear to drink farewell at Pavilion Long?
Do not sing your heart-breaking song!
While old, I have no tears to shed.

Your sail goes fast when wind is high;
Amid green waves it's lost to my eye.
When will messengers bring me word?
Summer wind brings no message-bearing bird.

CHEN YUYI

TUNE: DREAM OF A FAIR MAIDEN
MOORING AT THE FOOT OF MOUNT MING

Fish dance with dragons on the tide
To mourn over the poet drowned by riverside.
By riverside
States rise and fall,
Waves level all.

Without wine the Dragon Boat Day is passed in vain;
I moor my boat by riverside to watch the rain.
To watch the rain,
A lonely white-haired man at last
Comes to lakeside to mourn over the past.

TUNE: SILK-WASHING STREAM

The evening bell bids adieu after the crows;
East of the folded screen the railing's shadow grows.
Lying, I see the lonely crane on the wind fly.

I rise and dance in moonlight with a cup of wine;
The autumn sky's like water and wine like the sky.
Who'd drink with me since gone is the poet divine?

ZHANG YUANGAN

TUNE: ROUGED LIPS

Deep, deep, clear night so deep,
Flowers fall 'neath the eaves, in the dark crickets weep.
Curtains so chill,
Incense rises around the screen, atop its hill.

I dislike the message-bearing wild geese:
Their feeling as shallow as autumn cloud would freeze.
To whom may I my letter confide?
Lonely, I can only put it aside,
Forgetting I have former promise to keep.

TUNE: BUDDHIST DANCERS

When spring comes and goes, we grow old;
Though older than the young, are we less bold?
Drunk, the same fiery zeal we'll show.
What matters if white beard should grow!

I dance with flowers pinned in the hair;
I am master no matter where.
Wine cup in hand, I ask spring to stay.
Be not laughed at by flowers gay!

Lü Weilao

TUNE: SONG OF GOOD EVENT

I've crossed the river in flying snow,
And moored my boat by the Bridge of Red Rails, so
I tell you with my sail nothing goes wrong,
And send you two hand-written lines not long.

From now on I'll stay in South Tower from day to day,
And since then my hair will turn grey.
Who would write verse with me and share my cup of wine?
Can such life justify the books I've read line by line?

Deng Su

TUNE: EVERLASTING LONGING

The hills near by
And mountains high
Extend with misty water as far as the sky;
The longing maple leaves turn to red dye.

Chrysanthemums sigh;
Chrysanthemums die.
You don't come back when wild geese westward fly,
A screen of breeze and moonlight left before my eye.

TUNE: EVERLASTING LONGING

Red flowers fly,
White flowers fly.
My husband left me when the vernal breeze passed by.
But won't come back with spring, Oh my!

Rain falls once more,
Snow falls once more.
Again in the twilight I lean against the door,
A lonely lamp dims the floor.

YUE FEI

TUNE: THE RIVER ALL RED

Wrath sets on end my hair,
I lean on railings where
I see the drizzling rain has ceased.
Raising my eyes
Towards the skies,
I heave long sighs,
My wrath not yet appeased.
To dust is gone the fame achieved in thirty years;
Like cloud-veiled moon the thousand-mile land disappears.

Should youthful heads in vain turn grey,
We would regret for aye.

Lost our capitals,
What a burning shame!
How can we generals
Quench our vengeful flame!
Driving our chariots of war, we'd go
To break through our relentless foe.
Valiantly we'd cut off each head;
Laughing, we'd drink the blood they shed.
When we've reconquered our lost land,
In triumph would return our army grand.

Li Shi

Tune: Riverside Daffodils

All quiet, sparse are mist-veiled willow trees;
In painted bower a flute wafts with the breeze.
She leans on rails. Who calls "Rosette" in a voice low,
When incense burnt, to bed she wants to go?
The water clock shows it's midnight.

She waits for him to come; just come, again he'll go,
Leaving the square courtyard steeped in moonlight.
East of the white-washed wall a small bridge arches low.
Rising in the shade of flowers, she tries
To catch with her fan flitting fireflies.

KANG YUZHI

TUNE: TELLING INNERMOST FEELING
THE ANCIENT CAPITAL RECALLED

Where ancient palaces stood, now ruins stand;
Foxes and hares in throng haunt the waste land.
Past splendor turns into dreams of spring,
Leaving old grief for the modern to sing.

Don't mount the Merry-Making Plain!
From shedding tears can you refrain?
Down in the western sky
The setting sun goes;
Southward the wild geese fly,
But eastward River Wei still flows.

TUNE: EVERLASTING LONGING
ON WEST LAKE

The southern crest,
The northern crest,
The shimmering lake's veiled in haze from east to west;
Spring causes me unrest.

Deep deep your love,
Deep deep is mine.
My painted carriage's light and your horse fine,
Going nine miles, we meet beneath the pine.

TUNE: SONG OF DIVINATION

Clouds rise over river mouth with rising tide;
The trees see it ebb by the ferry side.
The tide is free to rise and flow;
So men are free to come and go.

Pavilions far and nigh
Bid welcome and goodbye.
Men have grown old who come from north, south, east or west;
But the pavilion still sees the tide without rest.

WANG YAN

TUNE: SONG OF GOLDEN DREAM

The mountains darken, overshadowed by cloud;
The cold weather thick with rain is not loud.
Red petals fall from a few pretty weeping trees.
Grieve not for flowers blown off by the vernal breeze!

Plodding out in straw cloak from day to day,
Coming back by ditchside pathway,
The peasants lead the hardest life from spring to fall.
What they need after all
Is but a bumper year
So dear!

Han Yuanji

TUNE: MORNING HORN AND FROSTY SKY
WRITTEN IN THE PAVILION AT FROWNING CLIFF

A frowning cliff against the sky
Commands the river from a thousand feet high.
On the two far-off browlike peaks with green congealed,
How much grief is revealed?
Can we express
It in excess?

Over angry waves swift blows wind drear;
Awake from wine, I hear flute songs from the frontier.
May I know where is the poet divine?
Beyond the green hills in a line,
Where mist and cloud combine.

TUNE: SONG OF GOOD EVENT
ON HEARING MUSIC AS AN ENVOY AT A BANQUET IN THE LOST CAPITAL

The Pond of Green Congealed looks as of old,
But now I find pipes and strings sad and cold.
How many old musicians still sing today?
Their songs but turn my hair from black to grey.

Where reigns spring grief, there apricot can't go;
Only in mist-veiled field can its flowers blow.
The lonely Royal Moat murmurs around
As human sobbing sound.

ZHU SHUZHEN

TUNE: PURE SERENE MUSIC
A SUMMER DAY ON THE LAKE

Annoying mist and enticing dew
Retain me for a while with puzzling view.
Hand in hand, we stroll by the Lake of Lotus Flower;
A sudden rain drizzles into a shower.

Fond to be silly, I care not for others, never.
Undoffed, I lie down with my breast against his chest.
What can I do when comes the time to sever?
Indolent when back, by my dresser I won't rest.

TUNE: AT THE GOLDEN GATE
MID-SPRING

Half spring has passed,
The view awakes a sorrow vague and vast.
Unoccupied, I lean on all twelve balustrades,
But Heaven cares not if my sorrow fades.

Although the sun is warm and the breeze fair,
I envy orioles and swallows in pair.
When courtyard flowers fall, I won't uproll the screen;
My heart would break when green grass can't be seen.

TUNE: FASCINATING EYES

In late spring days the gentle breeze
Plays with the slender willow trees;
Fragrance permeats the flowery pathway.
After the clear, bright Mourning Day,
How can I bear to think of bygone hours
Now clouds have veiled my crimson bower?

I wake from nap to hear the happy orioles sing.
Where will their songs evoke the grief of spring?
In willows' shade,
By balustrade
Of the Crabapple Bower,
Amid apricot flowers.

TUNE: BUTTERFLIES IN LOVE WITH FLOWERS
FAREWELL TO SPRING

Thousands of willow twigs beyond my bower sway;
They try to retain spring, but she won't stay
For long and goes away.
In vernal breeze the willow down still wafts with grace;
It tries to follow spring to find her dwelling place.

Hills and rills greened all over, I hear cuckoos sing;
Feeling no grief, why should they give me a sharp sting?
With wine cup in hand, I
Ask spring who won't reply.
When evening grizzles,
A cold rain drizzles.

TUNE: SHORTENED FORM OF MAGNOLIA FLOWER
GRIEF IN SPRING

Alone I stroll and sit,
Alone I chant and thyme, and still alone I sleep.
Standing, I feel unfit.
What can I do when cold spring torments me to weep!

Is grief beyond belief?
My neglected dress is half wet with tears in streams.
Illness comes after grief;
The cold lamp dying out, I can't even have dreams.

Zhao Yanduan

Tune: Measures at Court
The Refreshing Pavilion Inaugurated

The sky-scraping pine-tree holds the moon up;
A riot of fallen leaves startles wild geese.
Glistening dew looks like a brimming cup;
Laden with cloud, my sleeves can't flap with ease.

In southern scenic spot
Girt with blue stream and peak,
Maple leaves redden half the creek.
A roamer tired should go back to his cot,
In this pavilion he may lie
To watch the cold blue sky.

TUNE: ROUGED LIPS
MEETING WITH AN OLD FRIEND ON THE WAY

Languid at the earth's end,
I relive the bygone days when I meet an old friend.
So soon I part with you.
Can I bear to sing the song of adieu?

A roamer in an alien land,
To another roamer I wave my hand.
With baseless grief, I turn my head
To hear the cicada sings;
I see the setting sun red
Through their dark wings.

TUNE: SONG OF DIVINATION

The new moon looks like an eyebrow;
It's unwilling to be round now.
I can't bear to see the red bean
As lovesick tears will not be seen.

All day I break peach's inner part;
Like its core you're deep in my heart.
Two flowers severed by the wall
Will be united after all.

YAO KUAN

TUNE: SONG OF HAWTHORN
LOVE AT FIRST SIGHT

You're like the dust by the roadside;
I'm willow down on rivershore.
We meet while wafting far and wide,
But I can find your trace no more.

Your face is drunk with vernal breeze,
Like autumn rain my tearful eyes.
After we parted, tell me please,
Are you longing for me with sighs?

Lu You

TUNE: RIPPLES SIFTING SAND
AT A FAREWELL BANQUET IN THE PAVILION OF FLOATING JADE

Green trees darken the Pavilion Long;
I drink adieu once and again.
Often I hate to hear the farewell song,
Not to say of the autumn day
When I'm to go far, far away.

Silk scarfs wet with tears flowing,
Each of us is broken-hearted.
How could a riverful of parting grief be parted?
Where could I find the river-barring iron chain
To stop the grief from overflowing!

TUNE: SONG OF GOOD EVENT
VIEWING THE SEA ATOP MUME FAIRY MOUNTAIN

Waving my sleeves, I go up western mountain high,
Its summit only one foot from the sky.
Cane in hand, I overlook the sea where appear whales,
And count one by one mist-veiled sails.

I'm greedy to see clouds dance on the mirror bright;
On my way back it is twilight.
Thanks to the breeze among the pine-trees blowing,
I'm detained from home-going.

TUNE: PARTRIDGE IN THE SKY

Living between grey mist and setting sun,
I'm freed from all worldly cares one by one.
Drunk, I'll pass through
Groves of bamboo;
Books read, I would lie still
To contemplate the hill.

Why proud and bold?
Let me grow old
And wear, wherever I go, a smiling face!
Don't you know the Creator has the grace
To level heroes down to commonplace?

TUNE: MEASURES AT COURT

THE MUME BLOSSOM

Your lonely grace won't visit Vanity Fair;
Silent and sad, you do not care.
Like a wanderer you play your part
With an indifferent heart.

In moonlight by the stream,
With new verse and old dream,
I feel the grief your fragrance brings.
Uncared for by the vernal breeze on the wing,
You are the first to welcome spring.

TUNE: PHOENIX HAIRPIN

Pink hands so fine,

Gold-branded wine,

Spring paints the willows green palace walls can't confine.

East wind unfair,

Happy times rare.

In my heart sad thoughts throng;

We've severed for years long.

Wrong, wrong, wrong!

Spring is as green,

In vain she's lean.

Her kerchief soaked with tears and red with stains unclean.

Peach blossoms fall

Near deserted hall.

Our oath is still there. Lo!

No words to her can go.

No, no, no!

TUNE: EVERLASTING LONGING

With my face pale
And my hair grey,
I'm versed in letters, but to what avail?
I have leisure to sleep by day.

You want to receive praise
And audience of the king?
Glory and fame belong to youth since olden days.
Better go home as cuckoos sing!

TUNE: TELLING INNERMOST FEELING

Alone I rode a thousand miles long, long ago
To serve in the army on the frontier.
Now to riverside fortress in dream I can't go,
Outworn my sable coat of cavalier.

The foe not beaten back,
My hair no longer black,
My tears have flowed in vain.
Who could have thought that in this life I would remain
With a mountain-high aim
But an old mortal frame!

TANG WAN

TUNE: PHOENIX HAIRPIN

The world unfair,
True manhood rare.
Dusk melts away in rain and blooming trees turn bare.
Morning wind high,
Tear traces dry.
I'd write to him what's in my heart;
Leaning on rails, I speak apart.
Hard, hard, hard!

Go each our ways!
Gone are our days.
My sick soul groans like ropes of swing which sways,
The horn blows cold;
Night has grown old.
Afraid my grief may be descried,
I try to hide my tears undried.
Hide, hide, hide!

Fan Chengda

TUNE: SONG OF GOLDEN DREAM

Gazing on mume flowers,
I'll send love to the high towers,
Where fragrant clouds hang low and sweet blossoms blow,
What a pity that her tower's so high
That my orchid boat cannot come nigh!

Will the twin fish bring her word to my eye?
Will she write verse on a red autumn leaf?
I'll ask the stream to carry to her my lonely grief,
But eastward it will flow.
How can it westward go?

TUNE: THE MOON OVER THE TOWER

The balustrade
Of eastern bower casts its shade
In moonlight. In moonlight
The sky with breeze and dew is bright,
And apricot blossoms snow-white.

The sobbing golden dragon hastens the water clock
To drip beside the burner's smoke.
The silken curtain dim, candle flame forms a flower.
Candle flame forms a flower, a spring dream in an hour
Of southern riverside
And a sky far and wide.

You Cigong

TUNE: SONG OF DIVINATION

Spring wind and rain see you come nigh;
Spring wind and rain ask you to stay.
In haste over cups we say goodbye;
Spring wind and rain send you away.

Your tearful eyes are not yet dry;
Your green eyebrows frown in sorrow.
If you feel lovesick, do not go up high!
For wind and rain will rage tomorrow.

Yang Wanli

TUNE: SONG OF GOOD EVENT
VIEWING THE MOON AT THE VALE OF FLOWERS ON THE NIGHT
OF THE 13TH DAY OF THE 7TH MOON

Before it peeps into the bowers,
The moon shines first in the Vale of Flowers.
Not that in my study I see no moonlight,
But that a grove of bamboos keeps it out of sight.

It's only the thirteenth day tonight,
The moon is already jade-white.
If you want to see it shed silver rays,
Come on the fifteenth and sixteenth days.

Yan Rui

TUNE: DREAMLIKE SONG

What's wrong with flowers of the pear?
What's wrong with the apricot fair?
They are so red and white, so red and white
That the east wind is drunk with delight.
Do not forget,
Do not forget,
Tipsy on Peach Blossom Land, my sleeves were wet!

TUNE: SONG OF DIVINATION

Is it a fallen life I love?
It's the mistake of Fate above.
In time flowers blow, in time flowers fall;
It's all up to the east wind, all.

By fate I have to go my way;
If not, where can I stay?
If my head were crowned with flowers,
Do not ask me where are my bowers!

Zhang Xiaoxiang

TUNE: SILK-WASHING STREAM

On frosty day the sky seems steeped in water clear;
The brandished whip amid red banners whistles, hear!
The mist-veiled withered grass appears and disappears.

The Central Plain for miles burns with the beacon fire;
East of the watch tower I drink a cup of wine dire.
Drunken against the grievous wind, I shed sad tears.

TUNE: THE MOON OVER THE WEST RIVER
HALTED BY THE WIND AT THE FOOT OF THREE PEAKS

My boat is fully loaded with autumn hue,
The lake is paved for miles with shimmering view,
The God of Waves at sunset retains me to see
The scalelike ripples he sets free.

It's better if the wind abates tomorrow.
If not, I'll sleep in open air without sorrow.
In crystal palace is performed the rainbow dance.
Be sure to Lakeside Tower we advance.

TUNE: SONG OF DIVINATION

The wind spreads on the isle a fragrant smell;
The sun sets o'er the ferry with a willow tree.
I come near lotus leaves outspread pellmell.
But where is she who gathers lotus seed with glee?

Alone I lean against the tower high,
And I would talk to the lotus flower.
But what can I do now it won't reply
But turns and sheds red petals in shower?

Xin Qiji

TUNE: GROPING FOR FISH

How much more can spring bear of wind and rain?
Too hastily it will leave again.
Lovers of spring would fear to see the flowers red
Budding too soon and fallen petals too widespread.
O spring, please stay!
I've heard it said that sweet grass far away
Would stop you from seeing your returning way.
But I've not heard
Spring say a word.

Only the busy spider weaves
Webs all day long by painted eaves
To keep the willow down from taking leave.

Could a disfavored consort again to favor rise?
Could beauty not be envied by green eyes?
Even if favor could be bought back again,
To whom of this unanswered love can she complain?
Do not dance then!
Have you not seen
Both plump and slender beauties turn to dust?
Bitter grief is just
That you can't do
What you want to.
Oh, do not lean
On overhanging rails where the setting sun sees
Heartbroken willow trees!

TUNE: BUDDHIST DANCERS
WRITTEN ON THE WALL OF ZAOKOU, JIANGXI

Below the Gloomy Terrace flow two rivers clear.
How many tears of refugees are swallowed here!
I gaze afar on land long lost in the northwest,
Alas! I see but mountain crest on mountain crest.

Blue mountains can't stop water flowing;
Eastward the river keeps on going.
At dusk it makes me weep
To hear partridges in mountains deep.

TUNE: SLOW SONG OF ZHU YINGTAI
LATE SPRING

Ever since we parted
At Ferry of Peach Leaf,
The willow-darkened southern bank's been drowned in grief.
I dread to go upstairs again;
Nine days in ten are filled with wind and rain.
So, broken-hearted,
I see red petals fall one by one,
Uncared for, and there's none
To plead with orioles singing all the day long
To still their song.

Peering at flowered hairpin on my head,
I take it down to count the petals red
So that I may anticipate
His returning date,
Till lamplight flickers on my curtained bed.
Words choked in my dream upon
My lips: "Oh, grief has come with spring, I say,
Now spring is gone,
Why won't it carry grief away?"

TUNE: PURE SERENE MUSIC

The thatched roof slants low,
Beside the brook green grasses grow.
Who talks with drunken Southern voice to please?
White-haired man and wife at their ease.

East of the brook their eldest son is hoeing weeds;
Their second son now makes a cage for hens he feeds.
How pleasant to see their spoiled youngest son who heeds
Nothing but lies by brookside and pods lotus seeds!

TUNE: PURE SERENE MUSIC
PASSING A LONELY NIGHT AT BOSHAN

Around the bed run hungry rats;
In lamplight to and fro fly bats.
On pine-shaded roof the wind and shower rattle;
The window paper scraps are heard to prattle.

I roam from north to south, from place to place,
And come back with grey hair and wrinkled face.
I woke up in thin quilt on autumn night;
The boundless land I dreamed of still remains in sight.

TUNE: THE MOON OVER THE WEST RIVER
HOME-GOING AT NIGHT FROM THE YELLOW SAND BRIDGE

Startled by magpies leaving the branch in moonlight,
I hear cicadas shrill in the breeze at midnight.
The ricefields' sweet smell promises a bumper year;
Listen, how frogs' croaks please the ear!

Beyond the clouds seven or eight stars twinkle;
Before the hills two or three raindrops sprinkle.
There is an inn beside the village temple. Look!
The winding path leads to the hut beside the brook.

TUNE: THE MOON OVER THE WEST RIVER
WRITTEN AT RANDOM

Drunken, I'd laugh my fill,
Having no time to be grieved.
Books of the ancients may say what they will;
They cannot be wholly believed.

Drunken last night beneath a pine tree,
I ask if it liked me so drunk.
Afraid it would bend to try to raise me,
"Be off!" I said and pushed its trunk.

TUNE: CONGRATULATIONS TO THE BRIDEGROOM

That I should have aged so!
And my fellows, alas! how many still remain?
Life spent with naught to show
But hair turned silvery in vain.
Yet with a smile I part
With all that is mundane,
Whereof nothing gladdens the heart.
Charming are mountains green.
I would expect the feeling to be
Mutual, for we
Are somewhat alike, in mood and mien.

As I sit at the east window, goblet in hand,

My thoughts go to that poet of Peach Blossom Land,

Who bemoaned scattered friends under towering cloud.

He was the philosophic drinker true,

Unlike those who

Of fickle fame felt proud.

I turn back crying;

An angry blast be raised and dark clouds flying!

It matters little I can't see the men of old;

Rather a pity they cannot see me!

But even my contemporaries, all told,

How many of them really know me?

But two or three.

TUNE: SONG OF UGLY SLAVE
WRITTEN ON THE WALL ON MY WAY TO BOSHAN

While young, I knew no grief I could not bear;
I'd like to go upstair.
I'd like to go upstair
To write new verses with a false despair.

I know what grief is now that I am old;
I would not have it told.
I would not have it told,
But only say I'm glad that autumn's cold.

TUNE: PARTRIDGE IN THE SKY

While young, beneath my flag I had ten thousand knights;
With these outfitted cavaliers I crossed the river.
The foe prepared their silver shafts during the nights;
During the days we shot arrows from golden quiver.

I can't call those days back
But sigh over my plight;
The vernal wind can't change my hair from white to black.
Since thwarted in my plan to recover the lost land,
I'd learn from neighbors how to plant fruit trees by hand.

TUNE: SONG OF DIVINATION

The hard may not be strong,
While the soft may last long
Look into my open mouth if you think me wrong:
The teeth are lost before the tongue.

Side teeth all gone, behold!
I lose a middle one anew.
I tell the young not to laugh at the old;
I'll pass through the dog's hole with you.

TUNE: WATER DRAGON CHANT
ON RIVERSIDE TOWER AT JIANKANG

The southern sky for miles and miles in autumn dye
And boundless autumn water spread to meet the sky.
I gaze on far-off northern hills
Like spiral shells or hair decor of jade,
Which grief or hatred overfills.

Leaning at sunset on balustrade
And hearing a lonely swan's song,
A wanderer on southern land,
I look at my precious sword long,
And pound all the railings with my hand,
But nobody knows why
I climb the tower high.

Don't say for food
The perch is good!
When west winds blow,
Why don't I homeward go?
I'd be ashamed to see the patriot,
Should I retire to seek for land and cot.
I sigh for passing years I can't retain;
In driving wind and blinding rain
Even an old tree grieves.
To whom then may I say
To wipe my tears away
With her pink handkerchief or her green sleeves?

TUNE: SPRING IN PEACH GROVE

"Just a round trip of three hundred *li*,
Be back in five days," she asked me.
Now I am overdue one day,
Which must mean for her long hours of delay.

"Giddap!" My galloping horse seems too slow,
For impatient I grow.
I shout to a passing magpie,
"Go quick! Tell her I'm coming. Fly!"

TUNE: THE HIGHEST TOWER

I am old now.
Do I care for wealth and rank the world prizes?
Wealth and rank would lead to crisis.
Mu left the king who neglected to serve him wine,
And Tao would not bow for his stipend but resign.
Master Mu,
Prefect Tao,
I'll learn from you.

I'll build a garden called "Recluse"
And a pavilion where I may do what I choose.
I'll drink at leisure
And chant with pleasure.
Land changes hands from year to year in north and south.
How many spoonfuls could one put at once in his mouth?
Stop your old song!
Do not tell me what's right or wrong!

CHEN LIANG

TUNE: SONG OF GOOD EVENT
MUME BLOSSOMS

Two or three branches bright
Pierce through the misty green of twilight,
And slant under the eaves towards the maid
Playing on flute of jade.

Passing over wood and pool, waterlike moonlight
Plays with mossy stones in flowers' shade
I try to find in dreams the flying butterfly,
But I'm afraid its sweet fragrance has fled on high.

TUNE: BEAUTIFUL LADY YU
GRIEF IN SPRING

Light fleecy clouds floating in the east breeze
Bring drizzling rain down now and then.
To waterside pavilion swallows come again,
And pecking a clod of fragrant clay,
They fly with falling petals on the way.

The pathway strewn with crabapple blooms like brocade
Still shows slender spring fade.
At dusk in the courtyard crows caw amid willow trees.
I remember my love, it seems,
Picking pear blossoms with moonbeams.

Liu Guo

TUNE: SPRING IN A PLEASURE GARDEN
APOLOGY FOR DECLINING XIN'S INVITATION

How happy we should be
If I could be free
To cross the river in wind and rain,
Gorge a hog's leg and drink with you a cask of wine!

But Bai, Lin, Su, three poets, did retain
Me from going. Su said, "See West Lake, rain or shine,
Like Beauty of the West,
Richly or plainly drest!"
But Bai and Lin turned their head
Down or up,
And only drank till their faces turned red,
And filled again their cup.

Bai said, "It's better to
Visit the Heavenly Bamboo,
Where picturesque tower stands proud,
Two crisscrossed creeks flow east and west;
And southern peak and northern crest
Command high and low floating cloud."
Lin said, "It's not so good as Lonely Hill
With its mume flowers in full bloom,
Their fragrance floating in the gloom.
Why not decline
Xin's invitation till the day turns fine?
Here and now let's enjoy our fill!"

TUNE: SONG OF IMMORTALS

FAREWELL TO MY LOVE

It's easy to get drunk with wine of adieu.

Turning my head, I find thirty miles out of view.

My steed won't stop but fly from mile to mile;

I hold its halter for a while,

And sit down for a while.

What can I do when severed by hills and rills from you!

Though glorious task should be undertaken,

How can love be forsaken?

The streamer of mist-veiled wine shop slants away.

I may forward go,

Or I may stay.

To go or stay is for you as for me the same woe.

TUNE: SONG OF WAFTING FRAGRANCE
VISITING AN OLD LOVE WITHOUT SEEING HER

Her window clear and fair,
I guess she can't be there.
Over the incense burner her doffed clothes lie;
In fragrance they seem to vie.

In such a haste she went away
That she forgot to cover her mirror of brass.
I have not come here many, many a day.
How unlucky I am, alas!

TUNE: DRUNK IN TIME OF PEACE A FAIR ZITHER PLAYER

With heart and mind aspiring high,
With eyebrows long and forehead dark,
In moonlit bower to play on zither I try.
O vernal wind, O hark!

I think of you, I long for you, unseen
Even in my dream, O beloved of mine!
When incense warms the mica screen,
What can I do when I'm awake from wine?

TUNE: SONG OF MORE SUGAR
PASSING BY WUCHANG AGAIN

Reeds overspread the small island;
A shallow stream girds the cold sand.
After twenty years
I pass by the Southern Tower again.
How many days have passed since I tied my boat
Beneath the willow tree! But Mid-Autumn Day nears.

On broken rocks of Yellow Crane,
Do my old friends still remain?
The old land is drowned in sorrow new.
Even if I can buy laurel wine for you
And get afloat,
Could our youth renew?

Jiang Kui

TUNE: ROUGED LIPS
PASSING BY WUSONG IN THE WINTER OF 1187

The heartless swallows and wild geese
Fly away west of the lake with the cloud and breeze.
Peak on peak grizzles
In dread of evening drizzles.

Beside the Fourth Bridge, I
Would follow poets of days gone by.
How are they today?
Leaning on rails, I sigh.
High and low withered willows swing and sway.

TUNE: THE PRINCE RECALLED
WRITTEN AT PENG'S BOWER AT POYANG

Red maple trees bring autumn cool
Leaf on leaf to the pool.
I always share my boat
With clouds which float.
Roaming on Southern shore, I can't be free.
I long for you as you for me.
I know my singing mate must be
In this sad plight
Night after night.

TUNE: PARTRIDGE IN THE SKY
A DREAM ON THE NIGHT OF LANTERN FESTIVAL

The endless River Fei to the east keeps on flowing;
The love seed we once sowed forever keeps on growing.
Your face I saw in dream was not clear to my eyes
As in your portrait, soon I am wakened by birds' cries.

Spring not yet green,
My grey hair seen,
Our separation's been too long to grieve the heart.
Why make the past reappear
Before us from year to year
On Lantern Festival when we are far apart!

TUNE: TREADING ON GRASS
DREAMING ON THE RIVER

Light as a swallow's flight,
Sweet as an oriole's song,
Clearly I saw you again in dream,
How could you know my endless longing night?
Early spring dyed in grief strong.

Your letter broken-hearted,
Your needlework done when we parted,
And your soul secretly follows me.
Over the southern stream
The bright moon chills
A thousand hills.
How can your lonely soul go back without company?

TUNE: SILK-WASHING STREAM

Tipsy, my sleeves filled with breeze, I go on and on;
From sunny sky to withered grass eagles fly down.
My heart is broken to see the setting sun frown.

The grief dissolved in my four strings has oldened me;
From dreaming of you far away I can't be free.
Why should I have left you so soon, so hastily?

TUNE: SLOW SONG OF YANGZHOU

In the famous town east of River Huai
And scenic spot of Bamboo West,
Breaking my journey, I alight for a short rest.
The three-mile splendid road in breeze have I passed by;
It's now overgrown with wild green wheat and weeds.
Since Northern shore was overrun by Jurchen steeds,
Even the tall trees beside the pond have been war-torn.
As dusk is drawing near,
Cold blows the born;
The empty town looks drear.

The place Du Mu the poet prized,
If he should come again today,
Would render him surprised.
His verse on the cardamon spray
And on sweet dreams in mansions green
Could not express
My deep distress.
The Twenty-four Bridges can still be seen,
But the cold moon floating among
The waves would no more sing a song.
For whom should the peonies near
The bridge grow red from year to year?

Shi Dazu

TUNE: A PAIR OF SWALLOWS

Spring's growing old.
Between the curtains dust in last year's nest is cold.
A pair of swallows bank and halt to see
If they can perch there side by side.
Looking at painted ceiling and carved beams
And twittering, they can't decide.
Clipping the tips of blooming tree,
They shed
The shadow of their forked tails, which seems
To cleave its way through flowers red.

Along the fragrant way
Where rain has wetted clods of clay,
They like to skim over the ground.
Striving to be fleet in flight,
They return late to mansions red in twilight.
Having gazed their fill on flowers and willows drowned
In the shade, they should perch in fragrant nest,
Forgetting to bring message from the end of the sky.
Grieved, with eyebrows knit, the lady would rest
Her elbow on the painted balustrade and sigh.

TUNE: THE LOVER'S RETURN
REFLECTIONS IN MOONLIGHT

The moon and I are still the same, it seems;
The mume puts forth new buds as of yore.
The mume-like fair lady steeped in moonbeams
Is no longer in spring as the mume I adore.

Its fragrance wafts into my dreams;
Its pollen falls like dust apart.
The burden of love has broken my heart.
Amorous of lotus blooms the phoenix appears;
While my grief turns into tears.

TUNE: RIVERSIDE DAFFODILS

The grass roots turn green tender,
And willow twigs turn slender.
The old place revisited would break my heart:
The boat still lies across waves green,
On Red-railed Bridge in vain I lean.

Verse written on dreams of old
And new grief leaves me cold
On long long night in red quilt when we're far apart,
Don't let the useless moon
Shine on poor me alone!

TUNE: DOFFING THE PENDANTS

Strolling by flower-bed fine,

My robe fragrant with dew,

I'd confide to spring my verse new.

Often would I send my love,

But swallows won't carry it above

For him to read by pearl screen my clever line.

Deep, deep am I lovesick;

My sorrow is thick, thick.

How could I forget his whisper by lamplight?

Pear blossoms steeped in pale moon light,

I'd come in borrowed dream to gallery by flowers

To show him my sleeves wet with tears fallen in showers.

HUANG JI

TUNE: DREAM OF A FAIR MAIDEN

In autumn bleak
Plane trees are ripped of leaves, hearing the west wind shriek.
Hear the west wind shriek!
The wild geese scream forlorn;
And moans the broken horn.

The parting grief won't care for a wanderer's heart,
Year after year from golden flowers kept apart.
From flowers kept apart,
By courtyard on courtyard, your house unseen
Is veiled by screen on screen.

ZHANG JI

TUNE: THE MOON OVER MELON ISLET
WRITTEN AT VARIOUS-VIEWED TOWER

How much grief to see the autumn wind blows
By the riverside again!
Frontier grass skyward grows.
Where's the lost Central Plain?

Our heroes' tear on tear,
Though shed from year to year,
With the eastward-going river flows.
Only the moonshine
With my fishing line
On Melon Islet goes.

YAN REN

TUNE: TELLING INNERMOST FEELING
PARTING AT RIVERS ZHANG AND GONG

Your boat sets sail after a farewell song;
No grief on earth deeper appears.
The feelingless river eastward flows along,
The faster with my tears.

Though far away,
You oft turn your head still
To gaze on what you will.
Where would your broken heart stay?
Amid the riverside mume flowers,
In one of the small crimson bowers.

Liu Kezhuang

Tune: Spring in a Pleasure Garden
DREAMING OF A DECEASED FRIEND

Again we meet
In wineshop of the north
And the Bronze Bird Tower. Let the cook make mince-meat
Of the whale caught in eastern sea,
And stablemen bring forth
The fiery western steeds for you and me.
Heroes there are in the world, You and I.
Who else deserves drinking in our company?
But I will call
Warriors and swordsmen Who are not afraid to die.

Let the drums roll, and drink, drink deep!
But down to earth again: the cock wakes me from sleep.
So it is not to be, after all.
Great deeds might have been, had chance come my way.
It's too late now, I've lost my day.
Even a hero can only win honours high
Under a heroic sage.
Up! Let no future be overshadowed by
A nonheroic age!

TUNE: PURE SERENE MUSIC
ENJOYING THE MOON ON THE 15TH NIGHT OF THE 5TH MOON

Fine clouds swept away leave no trace
But a vast firmament with glass-colored face.
Drunk, I ride the jade dragon to tour on high
And clearly see a sealike azure sky

The fragrant crystalline palace is loud
With the immortals' song of rainbow cloud.
If they but spare some dew and breeze,
How the cooled human world would live with ease!

TUNE: PURE SERENE MUSIC
THE MOON GODDESS

The wind and tide run high;
I ride the Toad miles and miles up the sky.
I see the Moon Goddess dance with grace,
Unpowdered her pure face.

I tour the silver palaces with towers impearled;
Below I can't discern the mist-veiled world.
Drunk, the Moon Goddess shakes the laurel trees,
On earth blows a cool breeze.

TUNE: PURE SERENE MUSIC
THE FAIR DANCER OF A FRIEND

Her slender waist with girdle white
Can be lifted up on the palm of a hand.
A wind screen should be built to shield her on the height,
Lest she might fly away like a swan from the land.

Tender like fragrant jade,
Coquetry in her smile or frown may be displayed.
She flirts with her love, speaking by her eyebrows long,
Knowing not if her dancing steps are wrong.

TUNE: SONG OF DIVINATION

Petal on petal light as wings of butterfly,
Blossom on blossom red like scarlet dots small,
If flowers find no favor with the Lord on high,
How can they be so pretty one and all?

At dawn the trees in full blossom are fine;
At dusk few blooms on the branches remain.
If flowers find indeed favor divine,
Why are they blown down by strong wind and rain?

WU WENYING

TUNE: SILK-WASHING STREAM

I dreamed of the door parting me from my dear flower,
The setting sun was mute and homing swallows drear.
Her fair hands hooked up fragrant curtains of her bower.

The willowdown falls silently and spring sheds tear;
The floating clouds cast shadows when the moon feels shy;
The spring wind blows at night colder than autumn high.

TUNE: WIND THROUGH PINES

Hearing the wind and rain while mourning for the dead,
Sadly I draft an elegy on flowers.
Over dark green lane hang willow twigs like thread,
We parted before the bowers.
Each twig revealing
Our tender feeling.
I drown my grief in wine in chilly spring;
Drowsy, I wake again when orioles sing.

In West Garden I sweep the pathway
From day to day
Enjoying the fine view
Still without you.

On the ropes of the swing the wasps often alight
For fragrance spread by fingers fair.
I'm grieved not to see your foot traces, all night
The mossy steps are left untrodden there.

TUNE: SONG OF MORE SUGAR

Where comes sorrow? Autumn on the heart
Of those who part.
See the banana trees sigh without rain or breeze!
All say that cool and nice is night,
But I won't climb the height to see the moon bright.

My years have passed in dreams
Like flowers on the streams.
The swallows gone away, in alien land I still stay.
O willow twigs, long as you are,
Why don't you gird her waist and bar
Her way from going afar!

TUNE: DRUNK IN PEACH GROVE
FOR LU THE FLUTIST

We made merry by Sandy Stream on olden day,
When you were young and gay.
You blew your flute wafting to the moon with the breeze,
And flew with cloud and wild geese.

Surprised how stars on high
And things below have changed, I sigh.
We look at each other with temples grey.
In broken-hearted royal garden grass grows drear;
Leaning on rails, we wait for one never to appear.

LIU CHENWENG

TUNE: GREEN WILLOW TIPS

Tartar steeds in blankets clad,
Tears shed from lanterns 'neath the moon,
Spring has come to a town so sad.
The flutes playing a foreign tune
And foreign drumbeats in the street
Can never be called music sweet.

How can I bear to sit alone by dim lamplight,
Thinking of northern land now lost to sight
With palaces steeped in moonlight,
Of southern capital in days gone by,
Of my secluded life in mountains high,
Of the sea's grief for seeing heroes die!

ZHOU MI

TUNE: GLAD TO HEAR MAGPIES
WATCHING THE TIDAL BORE FROM SOUTHERN HILL

The sky with water blends,
The river dyed in autumn hue extends.
Snow-crowned hills and dragons rise from the deep;
Swift wind blows the sea up like a wall steep.

Blue dots seem to drip from mist-veiled hills,
The rainbow clouds redden the sky like grills.
Far away white birds mingle with sails white,
Beyond the stream we hear a flute at night.

WEN TIANXIANG

TUNE: CHARM OF A MAIDEN SINGER

Immense is universe,
Could dragons be imprisoned in pools so small?
How can we stay in wind and rain,
In grief and pain?
How can we bear
Cold crickets' chirp at the foot of the wall?
Where is the hero, spear in hand, crooning his verse?
And where's the talents' tower? All
Has vanished like snow in the air.
Seeing the river
Running forever,
We need not fear
No hero would appear.

Alas! like wafting leaves, you and I,
We come again to River Huai,
When the cold breeze begins to blow.
In the mirror we find a face oldened in woe,
But still unchanged is our loyal heart.
Now for the northern desert we start;
Turning our head,
We see a hairlike stretch of land outspread.
If my old friend should think of me,
Listen to the waling cuckoo on the moonlit tree!

WANG YISUN

TUNE: A SKYFUL OF JOY
THE CICADA

The cicada transformed from the wronged Queen of Qi
Pours out her broken heart from year to year on the tree.
It sobs now on cold twig and now on darkened leaves;
Again and again
It laments her death and grieves.
When the west window's swept by rain,
It sings in the air as her jasper pendant rings
Or her fair fingers play on zither's strings.
No longer black is now her mirrored hair.
For whom should its wings still be black and fair?

The golden statue steeped in tears of lead*
Was carried far away with plate in days of old.
Where can the cicada find dew on which it fed?
Its sickly wings are afraid of autumn cold,
And its abandoned form has witnessed rise and fall.
How many sunsets can it still endure?
Its last song is saddest of all.
Why should it sing alone on high and pure
And suddenly appear,
So sad and drear?
Can it forget the summer breeze
When waved a thousand twigs of willow trees?

---

*It was said that the golden statue in Han Palace shed leaden tears when it was removed with its golden plate full of dew.

Jiang Jie

Tune: A Twig of Mume Blossoms

MY BOAT PASSING BY SOUTHERN RIVER

Can boundless vernal grief be drowned in vernal wine?
My boat tossed by waves high,
Streamers of wineshop fly.
The Farewell Ferry and the Beauty's Bridge would pine:
Wind blows from hour to hour;
Rain falls shower by shower.

When may I go home to wash my old robe outworn,
To play on silver lute
And burn the incense mute?
Oh, time and tide will not wait for a man forlorn:
With cherry red spring dies,
When green banana sighs.

TUNE: BEAUTIFUL LADY YU

LISTENING TO RAIN

While young, I listen to rain in the house of song,
Overjoyed in curtained bed
Beside a candle red.
In prime of life I heard rain on the river long,
In lonely boat, when wailed wild geese
Beneath low clouds in western breeze.

Now that I listen to rain under temple's eave,
My hair turns grey
Like starry ray.
Who cares if men will meet or part, rejoice or grieve?
Can I feel joy or sorrow?
Let it rain till tomorrow!

TUNE: MORNING HORN AND FROSTY SKY

A shadow's seen
Past window screen.
Who comes to pluck flowers from my trees?
You may pluck what flowers as you please.
I do not know
To whom they'll go.

Those near the eaves
Are the best among green leaves,
To reach them you'd stand on tiptoe.
I tell you who pluck flowers: Don't you know
You will look fair,
If you put them aslant your hair?

Zhang Yan

TUNE: SONG OF FOUR WORDS

Orioles sing amid leafy trees green;
The breeze blows cloud-like willow down over the screen.
The east wind won't be blamed by blooms; it tries to bring
Their flying petals to overtake spring.

My neighbor's daughter greets me with a smile and says:
We should make merry when fine are the days.
Where can I find her tomorrow, at which hour?
In willows' shade before her bower.

TUNE: FLICKERING RED CANDLE
FOR SHAO THE PURE HEART

Across the stream I call for boat;
Where can I pick sweet blossoms afloat?
Spring beauty chiefly depends on flowers.
How few have not fallen in showers!

I will not miss the splendid bygone day,
But enjoy before the fallen reds are swept away.
Let me drink the old wine anew,
For several days you're out of view.
Sweet grass in willows' shade spreads out for you.

TUNE: SONG OF THE PEARL

No song is heard with my peach blossom fan in hand.

How much I am annoyed!

Don't you know bloom and gloom are not enjoyed?

Why don't you come back to our land?

Why don't you come back soon?

Don't sweep the yardful of fallen reds away!

Leave them there till the fickle lover may

Return and know

That he should grow

Old as spring bloom and waning moon!

许译中国经典诗文集

宋词三百首

许渊冲 译

五洲传播出版社　中华书局

序

为了更好，没有什么
清规戒律不可打破。

　　　　　　——贝多芬

美是最高的善；
创造美是最高的乐趣。

　　　　　　——叔本华

　　如果说"创造美是最高的乐趣"，那么，古代的中国
诗人可以算是享受过美好人生的了。因为早在两千多年以
前，中国就创造了美丽的《诗经》和《楚辞》；以后，中
国又创造了更美丽的唐诗和宋词。而在四者之中，最美丽
的要算后来居上的宋词。因为宋词所表达的思想感情，有
时似乎比唐诗还更深刻，更细致，更微妙。

　　词起源于隋代，全名是"曲子词"，"曲子"指音乐
曲调，"词"指唱词。"曲子"和"词"最初是一致的。
如敦煌曲子词中有一首《鹊踏枝》，词的上片是："叵
耐灵鹊多谩语，送喜何曾有凭据？几度飞来活捉取，锁上
金笼休共语。"曲子（词牌）和词写的都是喜鹊。但是一
支曲子可以填各种不同的唱词，后来，词的内容和词牌的
名字（除了词人自作的曲子以外）就没有多大关系了。例
如五代南唐冯延巳填了几首《鹊踏枝》："梅落繁枝千万
片"，"谁道闲情抛弃久"，"几日行云何处去"，等
等，除第一首有"枝"字外，都和喜鹊没有什么关系。

　　经过隋唐五代近四百年，词有了很大的发展。《全唐
五代词》只收录了词人一百七十多位，词二千五百多首；而
《全宋词》及《补辑》却收录了词人一千四百三十多位，词

更多达两万八百多首，几乎是前人总和的八倍。因为唐、宋两代是中国历史上经济繁荣、文化昌盛的时期，而当时西方正处在黑暗时代，所以唐、宋王朝是那时世界上最发达的国家。尤其是宋代，达官贵人蓄养家妓的风气，士大夫诗酒歌舞的生活，都胜过了前朝。从晏几道在《鹧鸪天》中写的："彩袖殷勤捧玉钟，当年拚却醉颜红。舞低杨柳楼心月，歌尽桃花扇底风。"也可见一斑了。

宋词的第一个高峰，是在宋仁宗的统治时期，代表人物是晏殊（晏几道的父亲）和欧阳修。他们做官做到宰辅大臣，写词侧重于反映士大夫阶层闲适自得的生活，以及流连光景、感伤时序的情怀，所用词调还是以晚唐五代文人常用的小令为主，词风近似南唐的冯延巳。例如晏殊的《浣溪沙》："一向年光有限身，等闲离别易销魂。酒筵歌席莫辞频。满目山河空念远，落花风雨更伤春。不如怜取眼前人。"词的上片说：人生是短暂的，充满了离别的忧伤，所以能够歌舞饮宴的时候，就及时行乐吧！下片又说：看到山河就怀念远方的人，加上花谢花飞、风风雨雨，更使人悲哀。但哀悼过去，梦想未来，有什么用呢？还不如珍重现在吧！从这首词可以看出，晏殊是个理性词人，他有一种掌握自己、节制感情、寻求安慰的办法。

晏殊节制感情，用的是消极的办法；欧阳修却更进一步，即使在苦难中，也能用对美好事物的欣赏来排遣他的忧愁，因此可以说，他用的是积极的办法。例如他写的《玉楼春》下片："离歌且莫翻新阕，一曲能教肠寸结。直须看尽洛城花，始共春风容易别。"这四句词典型地体现了欧阳修用情的态度。人总是有分有合的，花总是有开有落的，趁着人在花开的时候，要尽情享受现在的美好；等到人散花落的时候，再与春天告别，也不至于那么难分难舍，因为人毕竟已经享受了美好的春天，没有辜负春光，对得起自己了。欧阳修不但能欣赏大自然美好的那一面，人世间美好的那一面，而且对悲伤感慨的事物，也能看到可以欣赏、可以爱好的那一面。例如第四首《采桑子》："群芳过后西湖好，狼藉残红，飞絮濛濛，垂柳阑干尽日风。 笙歌散尽游人去，始觉春空。垂下帘栊，双燕归来细雨中。"西湖花落，柳絮飘扬，令人悲伤，但栏杆外的垂柳，整日在春风中摇摆，那婀娜悠扬的姿态，那经历过繁华之后，感到万紫千红总是空的意境，难道不是可以欣赏的么？那经历过斜风细雨，双双归来的燕子，不也是很可爱的么？因此，欧阳修的小令可以说是达到了宋词初期的最高境界。

严格说来，晏殊和欧阳修只是北宋前期婉约派的代表人物，而豪放派的代表却是与他们同时的范仲淹。范仲淹具有"先天下之忧而忧，后天下之乐而乐"的博大胸怀，曾率大军抗击西夏的武装侵略。他的词写边塞风光，如"四面边声连角起"，"羌管悠悠霜满地"；写军旅生活，如"燕然未勒归无计"，"将军白发征夫泪"；悲凉慷慨，如"酒入愁肠，化作相思泪"等。可惜他的词传世的不多，只能算是开了豪放派的先声。

范仲淹和晏、欧写的都是小令，每首只有几十个字，内容受到形式的限制；把小令发展成为长调的重要词人是柳永，柳词一首可以长达二百多字，内容更加开阔高远。晏、欧词里的感情主要是写"春女善怀"，柳词却转变为"秋士易感"了。晏、欧做过大官，用辞高雅，感情凝练；柳永却接近市民，用白话入词，善于铺陈。例如他的代表作《雨霖铃》就是层层铺叙的典型。他依次把送别的气氛（寒蝉凄切），地点（都门的长亭），以及过程

（留恋，催发，执手，相看，泪眼，无语，凝噎，直到念千里烟波等），一层层铺展开来，焦点由近而远，感情由浅入深。到了下片，更从个人的离别，想到自古以来普天下有情人的离别，从狭隘的个人遭遇，悟到人生聚散无常的哲理。但他并没有以理化情，而是进一步融情入景，把自己的离愁别恨，化成了"杨柳岸晓风残月"。这还不够，他又更进一步，推想到离别后惨不成欢的情况，"良辰好景虚设"，平常日子自然更难挨了。又如他的《忆帝京》也用平白的口语描写了迂回曲折的感情：先写别后失眠的痛苦（"展转数寒更，起了还重睡"），接着一转，想"回征辔"，但是无奈"已成行计"，就这样反反复复，思前想后，结果还是忍痛接受现实（"系我一生心，负你千行泪"）。后人冯煦评柳词说："曲处能直，密处能疏……状难状之景，达难达之情，而出之以自然，自是北宋巨手。"

概括地说，北宋前期，词坛上呈现着贵族词与平民词、雅词与俗词、小令与长调这样一种双峰对峙的局面。前者的高峰是欧阳修，后者的高峰是柳永。同期还有一位以写"云破月来花弄影"而出名的词人张先，他既写小令，又写长调，"适得其中，有含蓄处，亦有发越处"，出入于欧、柳两派之间，而以小令为主。到了北宋中期，王安石步武范仲淹，写了怀古咏史的豪放词《桂枝香》，要打破"诗言志"而"词言情"的题材分工，冲决"诗庄词媚"的风格划界，他成了承前启后的中坚人物。

北宋中期词坛的高峰是苏轼。他融会了儒道两家最美好的品格和修养，那就是"穷则独善其身，达则兼济天下"。在显达的时候，他有儒家"兼济天下"的理想；在失意的时候，他有道家超脱旷达的胸怀。这体现在他的

《沁园春》中："用舍由时，行藏在我。"这两句词概括了中国古代知识分子的人生哲学。苏轼是北宋词坛豪放派的代表人物。关于"豪放"，陆游说他"不喜剪裁以就声律"，是说他的性情不受束缚；刘熙载说："若其豪放之致，则时与太白为近。"是指他的风格。他豪放词的代表作是《念奴娇•赤壁怀古》，这首词是他贬谪到黄州时写的，但他却把个人的忧伤感慨，融合到广大开阔的自然景色之中，融合到古往今来的历史潮流之中；于是他的感慨，就不只是个人的成败得失，而是千古风流人物的盛衰荣辱；他不把个人的忧患看得那么沉重，因为古今有多少人物和他在一起分担了这些盛衰兴亡的感慨，他就借古人的酒杯，浇自己的块垒。词里有他政治理想落空的忧伤，但他并没有被忧伤压倒，而是让自然景色、让江水和明月来替他分忧；他甚至和江月融合为一，在"浪淘尽千古风流人物"的大江看来，在见过多少盛衰兴亡的明月看来，个人的成败得失算得了什么？就是这样，他以理化情，摆脱了忧伤的束缚，而这首词也成了豪放派的名作。

　　苏轼不但写豪放词，他写的婉约词也与前人不同。前人抒发的感情，不外乎伤春、悲秋、离别、相思，描写的女性总有点朦胧，有点概念化；到了柳永，他描写的景物是眼中所见的景物，描写的女性是现实生活中他爱过的女性，比前人进了一步，但他并不能摆脱利害得失和感情的束缚；只有苏轼，才把词当成言志抒情的工具，用词的形式表达诗的传统题材，咏史怀古，谈政论事，山水田园，赠答伤悼，"无意不可入，无事不可言"。他词中的女性也没有一般婉约词中的脂粉之气，卑顺之态，绸缪之情，宛转之辞，并不止于吟风玩月，而是往往寓有深意。例如他的《洞仙歌》中的花蕊夫人，丝毫不给人轻佻感，一片晶莹，显示了词人理想的境界，"冰肌玉骨"体现了词人理想的品格。又如他的《贺新郎》上片写一个高洁绝俗的美人，下片写群芳谢后才开的石榴花；美人幽雅独处，榴花不屑与浮花浪蕊为伍，这婉转隐约地写出了词人的不遇之感，可以说是词中的《离骚》，而苏词的特点就是"以诗为词"。即使他的山水田园词，如《浣溪沙·徐门石潭谢雨道上作》五首，以轻妙细腻的描写，平静地观照人生众相，虽然写的是日常生活的某个画面，却使人感到超越了单纯的写实，而具有广泛的象征性。《定风波》则更表现了对人生的达观态度。

如果说苏轼是"以诗为词"，那么苏门学士秦观写的却是"词人之词"。他的词中不必有什么寄托，什么理想，只有一种轻柔、细腻、婉转、微妙的感觉。如他的《浣溪沙》，上片写小楼上漠然、寒冷的感觉，写和秋天傍晚一般阴沉、萧索的春天早晨，写屏风上烟水朦胧的景色，写的是楼上的景物，却可以感到楼上人融入景中的情思。一般词人常把抽象的感情比作具体的景物，秦观却把具体的形象比作抽象的感情，在下片说"自在飞花轻似梦，无边丝雨细如愁"，这既用抽象的梦和愁来形容具体的花和雨，又反过来从实到虚，用帘外所见的"飞花"和"丝雨"来描写楼上人的幽怨，真是情景交融，迷离恍惚，耐人寻味。秦观不单是用眼中所见的实景，还用心中所想的虚景，来和词中抒发的感情结合。例如他的《踏莎行》，上片的"雾失楼台，月迷津渡"，写的并不是现实的景物；"桃源望断无寻处"，也是写内心幻灭的感觉；这几句写雾，写月，写桃源，和后面写的"杜鹃声里斜阳暮"的现实情景，是不相符合的，所以说是心中所想的虚景。下片说自己对家人亲友的怀念，想托驿使带信回去，这是写实；接着说不能回家的愁恨，是像砖石一样一块一块地堆砌起来的，这又是虚实结合。最后说"郴江幸自绕郴山，为谁流下潇湘去"，更是实事虚用，象征自己本应在家，为何贬谪异乡？思家怀旧，已经移情山水了。

集北宋婉约派大成、开南宋词坛先声的人物是周邦彦。他继承了柳永，但比柳更幽折多姿，又比秦观更深沉含蓄。他的代表作是《兰陵王·柳》，这首词托柳起兴，其实是写离情的。上片先写送别的地方：柳树成行，柳荫蔽地，连成一条直线。这表面上是泛写柳，实际上是写送别的背景。接着问城外隋堤上的柳树，柔条拂水，柳花飘绵，见过多少次送别的情景？这是借柳写离情。然后，"登临望故国，谁识京华倦客"？这时主人公才出场。"作客，一可悲；作客已久（"倦"），二可悲；望故乡而不见，三可悲；无人能了解（"识"），四可悲"（艾治平语）。写得多么深刻曲折！"长亭路，年去岁来，应折柔条过千尺！"这表面上是写爱惜柳树，内心却蕴藏着离别频繁、风尘奔走的感叹，写得多么情意深沉，含蓄不露！中片"闲寻旧踪迹"，写话别时旧地重临，但并不像柳永那样"执手相看泪眼"，也不像秦观那样"罗带轻分"，只写眼前看到的"离席"，耳中听到的"哀弦"，什么也没说，什么也没做，但离别之苦，却不言而喻。下片还是抒写离情，"斜阳冉冉春无极"一句，梁启超说："七字绮丽中带悲壮，全首精神提起。"这是借乐事写哀情，倍增其哀，因为下面接着回忆"月榭携手，露桥闻笛"等赏心乐事。如果和秦观的"杜鹃声里斜阳暮"以哀景写哀来比较，就可以看出秦、周的不同了。

北宋末年，金兵南侵，汴京失陷，徽宗、钦宗二帝被俘，高宗南渡，建都临安（杭州），开始了南宋血和泪、剑与火的时代。用血泪写词的有宋徽宗赵佶，他的《燕山亭》说："天遥地远，万水千山，知他故宫何处？怎不思量，除梦里有时曾去。无据，和梦也新来不做！"真是杜鹃啼血，一字一泪。用剑与火写词的有抗金名将岳飞。他的《满江红》光昭日月，气吞山河，是南宋前期豪放词的代表作。

南宋前期婉约派的代表，是中国古代最杰出的女词人李清照。她用口语写词，但比柳永高洁，比秦观素雅，比周邦彦清浅，辞淡于水，味浓如酒。她《醉花阴》中的"人比黄花瘦"，形象地写出了生离之苦；《声声慢》中的"寻寻觅觅"，又声泪俱下地写出了国破家亡、死别之痛。

南宋前期的爱国诗人陆游，既写豪放词，又写婉约词。他和欧阳修、苏轼一样，都是诗人写词。诗和词的分别，据缪钺说："诗显而词隐，诗直而词婉，诗有时质言而词更多比兴，诗尚能敷畅而词尤贵蕴藉。"陆游只有欧、苏诗人的气质，没有他们词人的眼光和笔法，所以陆词缺少婉转含蓄之类。他的豪放词多写壮志未酬的感慨，如《诉衷情》（当年万里觅封侯）；他的婉约词则写对前妻终生不忘的怀念，如《钗头凤》；他的托喻词不多，但《卜算子·咏梅》等却是佳作。

南宋豪放派的顶峰是辛弃疾。他和北宋苏轼齐名，两人的词都摆脱了那种绮罗香泽、剪红刻翠的作风，而抒写自己的怀抱志趣。苏轼既有儒家的用世之志，又有道家的旷达胸怀，但他的词抒旷达之怀多于言用世之志，而辛词却言志更多，甚至可以说是用生命来写词的，而他的志就是要收复失地。例如他南渡后写的第一首词《水龙吟·登建康赏心亭》，上片写沦陷区的山川在倾诉愁恨，说的是山，其实指的是人，真是情景交融。他空怀报国之志，只能在赏心亭上看落日西沉，听孤雁哀鸣；这些景语都是情语，"落日"暗喻南宋局势岌岌可危，"断鸿"暗喻自己孤立无援。他看刀抚剑，表现了空有杀敌立功之意，但"报国欲死无战场"，只能拍遍栏杆，愤愤不平。但醉生梦死的投降派，哪能理解他登高望远的感慨呢！下片他借历史典故抒写自己抑郁的情怀，失意的悲痛。他不能像张翰那样贪图家乡风味而弃官还乡，也不能像许汜那样没有忧国救世之心，只知购置田产房舍，而是像桓温一样担心虚度年华，不能实现收复失地之志。但是哪有红颜知己来揩干这英雄失意的眼泪呢？如果说苏轼是"以诗为词"，辛弃疾则多用典故，可以说是开了"以文为词"的先声。他写的婉约词《摸鱼儿》，梁启超说是"回肠荡气，至于此极。前无古人，后无来者"，其实也是借美人伤春来言志的。

南宋婉约派的代表是姜夔。沈义父说他"清劲知音"。所谓"清劲"，就是出奇制胜，不同凡俗；所谓"知音"，就是和周邦彦一样懂得音乐，炼字造句符合声律。他出奇制胜，如《扬州慢》中的"废池乔木，犹厌言兵"，连草木都反对入侵的金兵，人自然更不消说了；又如《点绛唇》中的"数峰清苦，商略黄昏雨"，用"清苦"二字形容云雾缭绕的山峰，用"商略"二字把山拟人化，仿佛山也在商量如何对付晚来的凄风苦雨，写得非常生动。他不同凡俗，喜欢写高洁的荷花和梅花，写荷如《念奴娇》中的"嫣然摇动，冷香飞上诗句"，把荷花比作含情脉脉的美女，启发了词人的诗兴，创意新奇。他写梅更自制了《暗香》和《疏影》二曲，前者以笛声兴起明月梅下的高士风致，塑造了自己如"野云孤飞"、飘然不群的形象；后者用玉龙哀曲总收客边篱角的佳人幽情，暗喻徽钦二宗被虏北去、后宫嫔妃葬身胡尘，隐现了他忧国伤时的悲哀，开了象征派的先声。他炼字造句，如《暗香》中"千树压西湖寒碧"的"压"字，《踏莎行》中"淮南皓月冷千山"的"冷"字，都将自然景物的静态美转化为动态美了。他词中的音乐美，杨万里说过："有裁云缝月之妙思，敲金戛玉之奇声。"可以和周邦彦媲美。缪钺说："周词华艳，姜词隽淡；周词丰腴，姜词瘦劲；周词如春圃繁英，姜词如秋林疏叶。"

　　吴文英和姜夔一样，都继承了周邦彦含蓄雕镂、重视格律的词风，但姜词不像周词那样勾勒描绘，而是弃貌取神；吴词却把周词的含蓄发展到了朦胧的地步。例如周词《蝶恋花》中的"月皎惊乌栖不定"，写的是明月和乌鸦之景，抒的却是离人感到月明星稀、乌栖不定的不眠之情，非常含蓄，是寓情于景。而姜词《踏莎行》中的"淮南皓月冷千山"，却既没有描绘月，也没有刻画山，只是摄取月和山的神韵，用了一个"冷"宇，其实是移词人之情于景。再看吴词《浣溪沙》的下片："落絮无声春堕泪，行云有影月含羞，东风临夜冷于秋。"前两句很像李商隐《锦瑟》中的名句："沧海月明珠有泪，蓝田日暖玉生烟。"也和李诗一样朦胧，一样难以猜测指的是谁。可能第一句的"春"是指词人，看见"落絮"而想起远离的情人，因此流泪；"春"也可能是指情人，词人看见"落絮"而想到她在流泪了；还可能是写景，"春"甚至是象征南宋！"落絮"是春天无声的眼泪。第二句容易些，"月"大约是指情人，词人看到"行云"就想到她含羞的表情；也不排斥是寓情于景，像白居易《长恨歌》中的"行宫见月伤心色"那样，这里就是"行云遮月含羞色"；"月"还可能象征南宋，那"云"就指敌人了。第三句大约是借景写情，词人感到凄凉，所以觉得春风比秋风更冷；也可能是去年秋天两人同游，所以不觉秋风之寒；还可能是暗写亡国之恨，所以一句之内时空交错，可以说是开现代派的先声了。吴文英还有一首《糖多令》，显示了词转化为曲的方向：一是加了衬字，如"纵芭蕉不雨也飕飕"中的"也"字；二是用了拆字的写法，如"何处合成愁？离人心上秋"，把"愁"拆成"秋"和"心"；后来《西厢记》把"奸"字拆成"女字边干"，就是一例，这说明了吴词对后人的影响。

南宋末期，婉约派四大家周密、王沂孙、蒋捷、张炎，都受了姜、吴的影响。周密注重音律，如《曲游春》中"正满湖碎月摇花，怎生去得"，最后四字平上去入，完全协律。王沂孙的咏物词"空绝古今"，用隐语暗喻来写深刻的亡国之恨，如《天香·咏龙涎香》，把朦胧词推到了隐晦的地步。蒋捷兼有婉约、豪放两派之长，词中抒发故国之思，山河之恸，被称为"长短句之长城"，对后世影响颇深。他的《霜天晓角》比吴词《糖多令》还更接近元曲。张炎是名将之后，词风承接周、姜两家，"兼有二家之长而无其短"，所作"备写其身世盛衰之感"。他的代表作《解连环·孤雁》，把象征词推向一个新的高度。最后，宋末词人还有"杀身成仁，舍生取义"的民族英雄文天祥，但他一死，南宋就灭亡了。

我译《宋词》和译《诗经》《楚辞》一样，尽量要保存原文的意美、音美、形美。首先，所谓意美，就是不但要译原文的表层形式，还更要译原文深层的内容，甚至言外之意。如果原文的内容和形式统一，那翻译比较容易；如果内容和形式有矛盾，那只好舍形式而取内容；如果原文的形式可以包括几种不同的内容，那就要选择最美的一种，所以说是意美。例如苏轼《念奴娇·赤壁怀古》中说："遥想公瑾当年，小乔初嫁了，雄姿英发。羽扇纶巾，谈笑间樯橹灰飞烟灭。故国神游，多情应笑我早生华发。"这几句中有三个问题：第一，"羽扇纶巾"指谁？是周瑜还是诸葛亮？郭沫若说指诸葛亮。从真（史实）的观点看来，《三国志》上说诸葛亮并没有参加赤壁之战，草船借箭和借东风都是《三国演义》编出来的，"羽扇纶巾"是三国时期的服饰，儒将都用，并不限于诸葛。从美的观点看来，凭空插入一个诸葛亮，会打破词情的上下连贯；如指周瑜，则"羽扇纶巾"正好说明"雄姿"，和小乔谈笑间，敌船灰飞烟灭，正好说明风流儒将，英姿焕发。第二，"樯橹"有人说是"强虏"，从美的观点看来，杀人不如放火，而赤壁主要是水上火攻。第三，"多情"指谁？"故国"指什么地方？有人说指苏轼夫人"神游"故乡；多数人认为凭空插入苏夫人不妥，应指周瑜"神游"赤壁；郭沫若更说是周瑜和小乔同游，画面更美。"多情"是谁？有人说是周瑜，有人说是词人自作"多情"，这句是倒装句，应该读成"应笑我多情，早生华发"。只有郭沫若力排众议，独辟蹊径，认为"多情"是指小乔，先和周瑜谈笑，又笑词人"早生华发"，两个"笑"字把小乔写活了，形象最美。所以我的译文采用郭说。

其次，所谓音美，是要尽可能传达原文的音韵、节奏、双声、叠韵等等。原文押韵，译文要尽可能押韵；原文有平仄，译文可以改为轻重音；原文多用双声字等，译文也可用双声词等。如李清照的《声声慢》词中多用凄戚之声，译文也尽可能用了凄戚之韵。

最后，所谓形美，包括句行的长短、句间的对仗、词句的复沓等。如吕本中《采桑子》的上片："恨君不似江楼月，南北东西。南北东西，只有相随无别离。"一句七字，二句四字，二、三句重复。七字对仗如晏殊《浣溪沙》中的名句："无可奈何花落去，似曾相识燕归来。"四字对句如秦观《鹊桥仙》中的"纤云弄巧，飞星传恨"。又如陆游《钗头凤》中的"一怀愁绪，几年离索，错，错，错！"既有对仗，又有词的重复。英文前言中举了蒋捷《一剪梅》不同的译文为例，可见高下。诗是绝妙好词的绝妙安排。在我看来，绝妙好词就是富有意美和音美的文字，绝妙安排就是富有形美或三美的安排。所以译文也应该是绝妙好词的绝妙安排。但原文和译文的绝妙好词并不是对等的，如上面说的"南北东西"和"无别离"，既有意美又有押韵的音美，在中文是绝妙好词，绝妙安排；译成英文，"西"和"离"并不押韵，没有音美，这就要译者妙手巧安排，译得使人知之、好之、乐之了。

这本《宋词三百首》内容以小令为主。翻译方法基本用的是优化法。如上面提到的吕本中《采桑子》上片的新旧译文如下：

    1. I regret you could not be like the full moon bright,

        Shining all night.

        Shining all night,

    It is ever in view and never out of sight. (旧译)

    2. I'm grieved to find you unlike the moon at its best,

        North, south, east, west.

        North, south, east, west,

    It would accompany me without any rest. （新译）

比较一下原文和新旧译，可以看出"江楼"二字都没有译，如果译成riverside tower or pavilion，那就音节太多，不是绝妙好词。旧译译成"满月",新译译为"最美满的月亮",意美不比"江楼月"差,音美和形美却胜过了对等的译文。"南北东西"旧译把空间换译成时间,新译把"南北"颠倒为"北南",可见原文的绝妙排列不一定是译文的绝妙排列,也要作适当的调整。新旧译都传达了原文的意美,但新译比旧译更形似,所以是更妙的好词。"只有相随无别离"的旧译说永远在望,新译说永远相伴不休息。新译的意美不在旧译之下,形似却在旧译之上,但若论词而不论译,旧译音美又在新译之上,所以只好让百花齐放了。贝多芬说过:"为了更好,没有什么清规戒律不可打破。"如果我们能用优化的译法,把中国的古典诗词译成富有意美、音美、形美的外文,那一定可以使世界文化变得更加光辉灿烂。

许渊冲

2003年4月18日

柳枝词

亭亭画舸系春潭，直到行人酒半酣。
不管烟波与风雨，载将离恨过江南。

点绛唇

感兴

雨恨云愁，江南依旧称佳丽。
水村渔市，一缕孤烟细。

天际征鸿，遥认行如缀。
平生事，此时凝睇，谁会凭栏意？

踏莎行

春色将阑，莺声渐老，红英落尽青梅小。
画堂人静雨蒙蒙，屏山半掩余香袅。

密约沉沉，离情杳杳，菱花尘满慵将照。
倚楼无语欲销魂，长空黯淡连芳草。

潘阆

酒泉子

长忆西湖，尽日凭栏楼上望。
三三两两钓鱼舟，岛屿正清秋。

笛声依约芦花里，白鸟成行忽惊起。
别来闲整钓鱼竿，思入水云寒。

酒泉子

长忆观潮，满郭人争江上望。
来疑沧海尽成空，万面鼓声中。

弄潮儿向潮头立，手把红旗旗不湿。
别来几向梦中看，梦觉尚心寒。

林逋

长相思

吴山青，越山青，
两岸青山相送迎，谁知离别情？

君泪盈，妾泪盈，
罗带同心结未成，江头潮已平。

昼夜乐

洞房记得初相遇，便只合长相聚。
何期小会幽欢，化作离情别绪？
况值阑珊春色暮，对满目乱花狂絮，
直恐好风光，尽随伊归去。

一场寂寞凭谁诉？算前言总轻负。
早知恁地难拚，悔不当时留住。
其奈风流端正外，更别有系人心处。
一日不思量，也攒眉千度。

雨霖铃

寒蝉凄切，对长亭晚，骤雨初歇。
都门帐饮无绪，方留恋处，兰舟催发。
执手相看泪眼，竟无语凝噎。
念去去千里烟波，暮霭沉沉楚天阔。

多情自古伤离别，更那堪冷落清秋节！
今宵酒醒何处？杨柳岸晓风残月。
此去经年，应是良辰好景虚设。
便纵有千种风情，更与何人说！

秋夜月

当初聚散，便唤作无由再逢伊面。
近日来不期而会重欢宴，向尊前闲暇里，
敛着眉儿长叹，惹起旧愁无限。

盈盈泪眼，漫向我耳边作万般幽怨。
奈你自家心下有事难见，
待信真个恁别无紫绊。
不免收心，共伊长远。

凤栖梧

伫倚危楼风细细，
望极春愁，黯黯生天际。
草色烟光残照里，无言谁会凭栏意？

拟把疏狂图一醉，
对酒当歌，强乐还无味。
衣带渐宽终不悔，为伊消得人憔悴。

少年游

长安古道马迟迟，高柳乱蝉嘶。
夕阳鸟外，秋风原上，目断四天垂。

归云一去无踪迹，何处是前期？
狎兴生疏，酒徒萧索，不似少年时。

少年游

参差烟柳灞陵桥，风物尽前朝。
衰杨古柳，几经攀折，憔悴楚宫腰。

夕阳闲淡秋光老，离思满蘅皋。
一曲阳关，断肠声尽，独自凭兰桡。

忆帝京

薄衾小枕凉天气，乍觉别离滋味。
辗转数寒更，起了还重睡。
毕竟不成眠，一夜长如岁。

也拟待却回征辔，又争奈已成行计！
万种思量，多方开解，只恁寂寞厌厌地。
系我一生心，负你千行泪。

范仲淹

苏幕遮

碧云天，黄叶地，秋色连波，波上寒烟翠。
山映斜阳天接水，荒草无情，更在斜阳外。

黯乡魂，追旅思，夜夜除非，好梦留人睡。
明月楼高休独倚，酒入愁肠，化作相思泪。

渔家傲

塞下秋来风景异，衡阳雁去无留意。
四面边声连角起。
千嶂里，长烟落日孤城闭。

浊酒一杯家万里，燕然未勒归无计。
羌管悠悠霜满地。
人不寐，将军白发征夫泪。

御街行

纷纷坠叶飘香砌，夜寂静，寒声碎。
真珠帘卷玉楼空，天淡银河垂地。
年年今夜，月华如练，常是人千里。

愁肠已断无由醉，酒未到，先成泪。
残灯明灭枕头欹，谙尽孤眠滋味。
都来此事，眉间心上，无计相回避。

定风波

罗绮满城春欲暮，百花洲上寻芳去。
浦映□花花映浦，无尽处，恍然身入桃源路。

莫怪山翁聊逸豫，功名得丧归时数，
莺解新声蝶解舞，天赋与，争教我辈无欢绪！

菩萨蛮

忆郎还上层楼曲，楼前芳草年年绿。
绿似去时袍，回头风袖飘。

郎袍应已旧，颜色非长久。
惟恐镜中春，不如花草新。

菩萨蛮

玉人又是匆匆去，马蹄何处垂杨路？
残日倚楼时，断魂郎未知。

阑干移倚遍，薄幸教人怨。
明月却多情，随人处处行。

菩萨蛮

哀筝一弄湘江曲，声声写尽湘波绿。
纤指十三弦，细将幽恨传。

当筵秋水慢，玉柱斜飞雁。
弹到断肠时，春山眉黛低。

江南柳

隋堤远，波急路尘轻。
今古柳桥多送别，见人分袂亦愁生，
何况自关情。

斜照后，新月上西城。
城上楼高重倚望，愿身能似月亭亭，
千里伴君行。

更漏子

锦筵红，罗幕翠，侍宴美人姝丽。
十五六，解怜才，劝人深酒杯。

黛眉长，檀口小，耳畔向人轻道：
"柳阴曲，是儿家，门前红杏花。"

诉衷情

花前月下暂相逢，苦恨阻从容。
何况酒醒梦断，花谢月朦胧？

花不尽，月无穷，两心同。
此时愿作，杨柳千丝，绊惹春风。

天仙子

水调数声持酒听，午醉醒来愁未醒。
送春春去几时回？
临晚镜，伤流景，往事后期空记省。

沙上并禽池上暝，云破月来花弄影。
重重帘幕密遮灯。
风不定，人初静，明日落红应满径。

木兰花

和孙公素别安陆

相离徒有相逢梦，门外马蹄尘已动。
怨歌留待醉时听，远目不堪空际送。

今宵风月知谁共？声咽琵琶槽上凤。
人生无物比多情，江水不深山不重。

晏殊

踏莎行

细草愁烟，幽花怯露，凭栏总是销魂处。
日高深夜静无人，时时海燕双飞去。

带缓罗衣，香残蕙炷，天长不禁迢迢路。
垂杨只解惹东风，何曾系得行人住？

踏莎行

祖席离歌，长亭别宴，香尘已隔犹回面。
居人匹马映林嘶，行人去棹依波转。

画阁魂消，高楼目断，斜阳只送平波远。
无穷无尽是离愁，天涯海角寻思遍。

浣溪沙

一曲新词酒一杯，去年天气旧亭台，
夕阳西下几时回？

无可奈何花落去，似曾相识燕归来。
小园香径独徘徊。

浣溪沙

小阁重帘有燕过，晚花红片落庭莎，
曲阑干影入凉波。

一霎好风生翠幕，几回疏雨滴圆荷？
酒醒人散得愁多。

浣溪沙

一向年光有限身，等闲离别易销魂。
酒宴歌席莫辞频。

满目山河空念远，落花风雨更伤春。
不如怜取眼前人。

蝶恋花

槛菊愁烟兰泣露，罗幕轻寒，燕子双飞去。
明月不谙离恨苦，斜光到晓穿朱户。

昨夜西风凋碧树，独上高楼，望尽天涯路。
欲寄彩笺兼尺素，山长水阔知何处？

清平乐

红笺小字，说尽平生意。
鸿雁在云鱼在水，惆怅此情难寄。

斜阳独倚西楼，遥山恰对帘钩。
人面不知何处，绿波依旧东流。

诉衷情

芙蓉金菊斗馨香，天气欲重阳。
远村秋色如画，红树间疏黄。

流水淡，碧天长，路茫茫。
凭高望断，鸿雁来时，无限思量。

滴滴金

梅花漏泄春消息，柳丝长，草芽碧。
不觉星霜鬓边白，念时光堪惜。

兰堂把酒留嘉宾，对离筵，驻行色。
千里音尘便疏隔，会有人相忆。

玉楼春

春恨

绿杨芳草长亭路，年少抛人容易去。
楼头残梦五更钟，花底离情三月雨。

无情不似多情苦，一寸还成千万缕。
天涯地角有穷时，只有相思无尽处。

离亭燕

一带江山如画，风物向秋潇洒。
水浸碧天何处断？霁色冷光相射。
蓼屿荻花洲，掩映竹篱茅舍。

云际客帆高挂，烟外酒旗低亚。
多少六朝兴废事，尽入渔樵闲话。
怅望倚层楼，寒日无言西下。

玉楼春

东城渐觉风光好，縠皱波纹迎客棹。
绿杨烟外晓寒轻，红杏枝头春意闹。

浮生长恨欢娱少，肯爱千金轻一笑？
为君持酒劝斜阳，且向花间留晚照。

欧阳修

长相思

蘋满溪，柳绕堤，
相送行人溪水西。回时陇月低。

烟霏霏，雨凄凄，
重倚朱门听马嘶。寒鸥相对飞。

诉衷情

清晨帘幕卷轻霜，呵手试梅妆。
都缘自有离恨，故画作远山长。

思往事，惜流光，易成伤。
未歌先敛，欲笑还颦，最断人肠。

踏莎行

候馆梅残，溪桥柳细，草熏风暖摇征辔。
离愁渐远渐无穷，迢迢不断如春水。

寸寸柔肠，盈盈粉泪，楼高莫近危栏倚。
平芜尽处是春山，行人更在春山外。

生查子

去年元夜时，花市灯如昼。
月上柳梢头，人约黄昏后。

今年元夜时，月与灯依旧。
不见去年人，泪湿春衫袖。

望江南

江南蝶，斜日一双双。
身似何郎全傅粉，心如韩寿爱偷香，天赋与轻狂。

微雨后，薄翅腻烟光。
才伴游蜂来小院，又随飞絮过东墙，长是为花忙。

望江南

江南柳，花柳两相柔。
花片落叶粘酒盏，柳条低处拂人头，各自是风流。

江南月，如镜复如钩。
似镜不侵红粉面，似钩不挂画帘头，长是照离愁。

玉楼春

尊前拟把归期说，欲语春容先惨咽。
人生自是有情痴，此恨不关风与月。

离歌且莫翻新阕，一曲能教肠寸结。
直须看尽洛城花，始共春风容易别。

玉楼春

别后不知君远近，触目凄凉多少闷！
渐行渐远渐无书，水阔鱼沉何处问？

夜深风竹敲秋韵，万叶千声皆是恨。
故欹单枕梦中寻，梦又不成灯又烬。

南歌子

凤髻金泥带，龙纹玉掌梳，
走来窗下笑相扶，爱道画眉深浅入时无？

弄笔偎人久，插花试手初，
等闲妨了绣功夫，笑问鸳鸯两字怎生书？

临江仙

柳外轻霜池上雨，雨声滴碎荷声。
小楼西角断虹明。
栏杆私倚处，待得月华生。

燕子飞来窥画栋，玉钩垂下帘旌。
凉波不动簟纹平。
水晶双枕畔，傍有堕钗横。

怨春郎

为伊家终日闷，受尽恓惶谁问？
不知不觉上心头，悄一霎，身心顿也没处顿。

恼愁肠，成寸寸。已恁莫把人萦损。
奈每每人前道着伊，空把相思泪眼和衣揾。

蝶恋花

庭院深深深几许？杨柳堆烟，帘幕无重数。
玉勒雕鞍游冶处，楼高不见章台路。

雨横风狂三月暮，门掩黄昏，无计留春住。
泪眼问花花不语，乱红飞过秋千去。

司马光

西江月

宝髻松松挽就，铅华淡淡妆成。
红烟翠雾罩轻盈，飞絮游丝无定。

相见争如不见，有情还似无情。
笙歌散后酒微醒，深院月明人静。

王安石

桂枝香

金陵怀古

登临送目，正故国晚秋，天气初肃。
千里澄江似练，翠峰如簇。
征帆去棹残阳里，背西风，酒旗斜矗。
彩舟云淡，星河鹭起，图画难足。

念往昔，繁华竞逐。
叹门外楼头，悲恨相续。
千古凭高对此，谩嗟荣辱。
六朝旧事随流水，但寒烟，衰草凝绿。
至今商女，时时犹唱，后庭遗曲。

浣溪沙

百亩中庭半是苔，门前白道水萦回。
爱闲能有几人来？

小院回廊春寂寂，山桃溪杏两三栽。
为谁零落为谁开？

南乡子

自古帝王州，郁郁葱葱佳气浮。
四百年来成一梦，堪愁。晋代衣冠成古丘。

绕水恣行游，上尽层城更上楼。
往事悠悠君莫问，回头。槛外长江空自流。

菩萨蛮

集句

海棠乱发皆临水，君知此处花何似？
凉月白纷纷，香风隔岸闻。

嗓枝黄鸟近，隔岸声相应。
随意坐莓苔，飘零酒一杯。

王安国

清平乐

留春不住，费尽莺儿语。
满地残红宫锦污，昨夜南国风雨。

小怜初上琵琶，晓来思绕天涯。
不肯画堂朱户，春风自在杨花。

减字木兰花

画桥流水，雨湿落红飞不起。
月破黄昏，帘里余香马上闻。

徘徊不语，今夜梦魂何处去？
不似垂杨，犹解飞花入洞房。

晏几道

临江仙

梦后楼台高锁，酒醒帘幕低垂。
去年春恨却来时，
落花人独立，细雨燕双飞。

记得小蘋初见，两重心字罗衣，
琵琶弦上说相思。
当时明月在，曾照彩云归。

蝶恋花

梦入江南烟水路，行尽江南，不与离人遇。
睡里消魂无说处，觉来惆怅消魂误。

欲尽此情书尺素，浮雁沉鱼，终了无凭据。
却倚缓弦歌别绪，断肠移破秦筝柱。

鹧鸪天

彩袖殷勤捧玉钟，当年拚却醉颜红。
舞低杨柳楼心月，歌尽桃花扇影风。

从别后，忆相逢，几回魂梦与君同！
今宵剩把银釭照，犹恐相逢是梦中。

生查子

长恨涉江遥，移向溪头住。
闲荡木兰舟，误入鸳鸯浦。

无端轻薄云，暗作帘纤雨。
翠袖不胜寒，欲共荷花语。

采桑子

秋来更觉销魂苦，小字还稀。
坐想行思，怎得相看似旧时？

南楼把酒凭肩处，风月应知。
别后除非，梦里时时得见伊。

清平乐

留人不住，醉解兰舟去。
一棹碧涛春水路，过尽晓莺啼处。

渡头杨柳青青，枝枝叶叶离情。
此后锦书休寄，画楼云雨无凭。

木兰花

秋千庭院重帘暮，彩笔闲来题绣户。
墙头丹杏雨余花，门外绿杨风后絮。

朝云信断知何处？应作襄王春梦去。
紫骝认得旧游踪，嘶过画桥东畔路。

玉楼春

雕鞍好为莺花住，占取东城南陌路。
尽教春思乱如云，莫管世情轻似絮。

古来都被虚名误，宁负虚名身莫负。
劝君频入醉乡来，此是无愁无恨处。

阮郎归

旧香残粉似当初，人情恨不如。
一春犹有数行书，秋来书更疏。

衾凤冷，枕鸳孤，愁肠待酒舒。
梦魂纵有也成虚，那堪和梦无？

浣溪沙

日日双眉都画长，行云飞絮共轻狂。
不将心嫁冶游郎。

溅酒滴散歌扇子，弄花熏得舞衣香。
一春弹泪说凄凉。

诉衷情

长因蕙草记罗裙，绿腰沉水熏。
阑干曲处人静，曾共倚黄昏。

风有韵，月无痕，暗销魂。
拟将幽恨，试写残花，寄与朝云。

点绛唇

花信来时，恨无人似花依旧。
又成春瘦，折断门前柳。

天与多情，不与长相守。
分飞后，泪痕和酒，占了双罗袖。

少年游

离多最是，东西流水，终解两相逢。
浅情纵似，行云无定，犹到梦魂中。

可怜人意，薄于云水，佳会更难重。
细想从来，断肠多处，不与这番同！

留春令

画屏天畔，梦回依约，十洲云水。
手捻红笺寄人书，写无限伤春事。

别浦高楼曾漫倚，对江南千里。
楼下分流水声中，有当日凭高泪。

思远人

红叶黄花秋意晚，千里念行客。

飞云过尽，归鸿无信，何处寄书得？

泪弹不尽当窗滴，就砚旋研墨。

渐写到别来，此情深处，红笺为无色。

王观

卜算子

水是眼波横，山是眉峰聚。

欲问行人去那边？眉眼盈盈处。

才始送春归，又送君归去，

若到江南赶上春，千万和春住！

苏轼

昭君怨

谁作桓伊之弄，惊破绿窗幽梦？

新月与愁烟，满江天。

欲去又还不去，明日落花飞絮。

飞絮送行舟，水东流。

醉落魄

离京口作

轻云微月，二更酒醒船初发。

孤城回望苍烟合。

记得歌时，不记归时节。

巾偏扇坠藤床滑，觉来幽梦无人说。

此生飘零何时歇？

家在西南，常作东南别。

南乡子

送述古

回首乱山横，不见居人只见城。

谁似临平山上塔，亭亭，迎客西来送客行？

归路晚风清，一枕初寒梦不成。

今夜残灯初照处，荧荧，秋雨晴时泪不晴。

水调歌头

明月几时有？把酒问青天。

不知天上宫阙，今夕是何年？

我欲乘风归去，又恐琼楼玉宇，高处不胜寒。

起舞弄清影，何似在人间！

转朱阁，低绮户，照无眠。
不应有恨，何事长向别时圆？
人有悲欢离合，月有阴晴圆缺，此事古难全。
但愿人长久，千里共婵娟！

念奴娇

大江东去，浪淘尽千古风流人物。
故垒西边，人道是三国周郎赤壁，
乱石崩云，惊涛裂岸，卷起千堆雪。
江山如画，一时多少豪杰！

遥想公瑾当年，小乔初嫁了，雄姿英发。
羽扇纶巾，谈笑间樯橹灰飞烟灭。
故国神游，多情应笑我早生华发。
人间如梦，一尊还酹江月。

西江月

世事一场大梦，人生几度秋凉。
夜来风叶已鸣廊，看取眉头鬓上。

酒贱常愁客少，月明多被云妨。
中秋谁与共孤光？把盏凄然北望。

西江月

照野涨涨浅浪，横空隐隐层霄。
障泥未解玉骢骄，我欲醉眠芳草。

可惜一溪风月，莫教踏碎琼瑶。
解鞍欹枕绿杨桥，杜宇一声春晓。

临江仙

夜归临皋

夜饮东坡醉复醒，归来仿佛三更。
家童鼻息已雷鸣，敲门都不应，倚杖听江声。

长恨此身非我有，何时忘却营营？
夜阑风静縠纹平。小舟从此逝，江海寄余生。

定风波

莫听穿林打叶声，何妨吟啸且徐行。
竹杖芒鞋轻胜马，谁怕？一蓑烟雨任平生。

料峭春风吹酒醒，微冷。山头斜照却相迎。
回首向来萧瑟处，归去！也无风雨也无晴。

少年游

润州作

去年相送，余杭门外，飞雪似杨花。
今年春尽，杨花似雪，犹不见还家。

对酒卷帘邀明月，风露透窗纱。
恰似姮娥怜双燕，分明照，画梁斜。

卜算子

黄州定惠院寓居作

缺月挂疏桐，漏断人初静。
谁见幽人独往来？缥缈孤鸿影。

惊起却回头，有恨无人省。
拣尽寒枝不肯栖，寂寞沙洲冷。

江城子

乙卯正月二十日夜记梦

十年生死两茫茫，不思量，自难忘。
千里孤坟，无处话凄凉。
纵使相逢应不识：尘满面，鬓如霜。

夜来幽梦忽还乡，小轩窗，正梳妆。
相顾无言，唯有泪千行。
料得年年肠断处，明月夜，短松冈。

蝶恋花

花褪残红青杏小，燕子飞时，绿水人家绕。
枝上柳棉吹又少，天涯何处无芳草！

墙里秋千墙外道，墙外行人，墙里佳人笑。
笑渐不闻声渐悄，多情却被无情恼。

生查子

诉别

三度别君来，此别真迟暮。
白尽老髭须，明日淮南去。

酒罢月随人，泪湿花如雾。
后月逐君还，梦绕湖边路。

阳关曲

中秋作

暮云收尽溢清寒，银汉无声转玉盘。
此生此夜不长好，明月明年何处看？

调笑令

渔父，渔父，江上微风细雨。
青蓑黄箬裳衣，红酒白鱼暮归。
归暮，归暮，长笛一声何处？

减字木兰花

琴

神闲意定，万籁收声天地静。
玉指冰弦，未动宫商意已传。

悲风流水，写出寥寥千古意。
归去无眠，一夜余音在耳边。

如梦令

题淮山楼

城上层楼叠巘，城下清淮古汴。
举手揖吴云，人与暮天俱远。
魂断，魂断，后夜松江月满。

李之仪

卜算子

我住长江头，君住长江尾。
日日思君不见君，共饮长江水。

此水几时休？此恨何日已？
只愿君心似我心，定不负相思意。

忆秦娥

用太白韵

清溪咽，霜风洗出山头月。
山头月，迎得云归，还送云别。

不知今是何时节？凌霄望断音尘绝。
音尘绝，帆来帆去，天际双阙。

黄庭坚

定风波

万里黔中一漏天，屋居终日似乘船。
及至重阳天也霁，催醉，鬼门关外蜀江前。

莫笑老翁犹气岸，君看，几人黄菊上华颠？
戏马台南追两谢，驰射，风流犹拍古人肩。

清平乐

春归何处？寂寞无行路。
若有人知春去处，唤取归来同住。

春无踪迹谁知？除非问取黄鹂。
百啭无人能解，因风飞过蔷薇。

鹧鸪天

黄菊枝头生晓寒，人生莫放酒杯干。
风前横笛斜吹雨，醉里簪花倒著冠。

身健在，且加餐。舞裙歌板尽情欢。
黄花白发相牵挽，付与世人冷眼看。

诉衷情

一波才动万波随，蓑笠一钩丝。
锦鳞正在深处，千尺也须垂。

吞又吐，信还疑，上钩迟。
水寒江静，满目青山，载月明归。

采桑子

投荒万里无归路，雪点鬓繁。
度鬼门关，已拚儿童作楚蛮。

黄云苦竹啼归去，绕荔枝山。
蓬户身闲，歌板谁家教小蛮？

望江东

江水西头隔烟树，望不见江东路。
思量只有梦来去，更不怕，江阑住。

灯前写了书无数，算没个人传与。
直说寻得雁吩咐，又还是，秋将暮。

卜算子

要见不得见，要近不得近。
试问得君多少怜？管不解多于恨。

禁止不得泪，忍管不得闷。
天上人间有底愁，向个里都谙尽。

满庭芳

山抹微云，天粘衰草，画角声断谯门。
暂停征棹，聊共饮离尊。
多少蓬莱旧事，空回首，烟霭纷纷。
斜阳外，寒鸦数点，流水绕孤村。

销魂，当此际，香囊暗解，罗带轻分。
谩赢得青楼，薄倖名存。
此去何时见也，襟袖上，空惹啼痕。
伤情处，高楼望断，灯火已黄昏。

江城子

西城杨柳弄春柔，动离忧，泪难收。
犹忆多情，曾为系归舟。
碧野朱桥当日事，人不见，水空流。

韶华不为少年留，恨悠悠，几时休？
飞絮落花时候一登楼。
便做春江都是泪，流不尽，许多愁。

江城子

南来飞燕北归鸿，偶相逢，惨愁容。
绿鬓朱颜，重见两衰翁。
别后悠悠君莫问，无限事，不言中。

小槽春酒滴朱红，莫匆匆，满金钟。
饮散落花流水各西东。
后会不知何处是，烟浪远，暮云重。

鹊桥仙

纤云弄巧，飞星传恨，银汉迢迢暗度。
金风玉露一相逢，便胜却人间无数。

柔情似水，佳期如梦，忍顾鹊桥归路？
两情若是久长时，又岂在朝朝暮暮？

减字木兰花

天涯旧恨，独自凄凉人不问。
欲见回肠，断尽金炉小篆香。

黛蛾长敛，任是东风吹不展。
困倚危楼，过尽飞鸿字字愁。

画堂春

落红铺径水平池，弄晴小雨霏霏。
杏园憔悴杜鹃啼，无奈春归。

柳外画楼独上，凭栏手捻花枝。
放花无语对斜晖，此恨谁知？

踏莎行

郴州客舍

雾失楼台，月迷津渡，桃源望断无寻处。
可堪孤馆闭春寒，杜鹃声里斜阳暮。

驿寄梅花，鱼传尺素，砌成此恨无重数。
郴江幸自绕郴山，为谁流下潇湘去！

浣溪沙

漠漠轻寒上小楼，晓阴无奈是穷秋。
淡烟流水画屏幽。

自在飞花轻似梦，无边丝雨细如愁。
宝帘闲挂小银钩。

阮郎归

湘天风雨破寒初，深沉庭院虚。
丽谯吹罢小单于，迢迢清夜徂。

乡梦断，旅魂孤，峥嵘岁又除。
衡阳犹有雁传书，郴阳和雁无。

虞美人

高城望断尘如雾，不见联骖处。
夕阳村外小湾头，只有柳花无数送归舟。

琼枝玉树频相见，只恨离人远。
欲将幽恨寄青楼，争奈无情江水不西流！

点绛唇

醉漾轻舟，信流引到花深处。
尘缘相误，无计花间住。

烟水茫茫，回首斜阳暮。
山无数，乱红如雨，不记来时路。

好事近

梦中作

春路雨添花，花动一山春色。
行到小溪深处，有黄鹂千百。

飞云当面化龙蛇，夭矫转空碧。
醉卧古藤阴下，了不知南北。

米芾

西江月

秋兴

溪面荷香粲粲，林端远岫青青。
楚天秋色太多情，云卷烟收风定。

夜静冰娥欲上，梦回醉眼初醒。
玉瓶未耻有新声，一曲请君来听。

浣溪沙

野眺

日射平溪玉宇中，云横远渚岫重重。
野花犹向涧边红。

静看沙头鱼入网，闲支藜杖醉吟风，
小春天气恼人浓。

赵令畤

蝶恋花

卷絮风头寒欲尽，坠粉飘香，日日红成阵。
新酒又添残酒困，今春不减前春恨。

蝶去莺飞无处问，隔水高楼，望断双鱼信。
恼乱横波秋一寸，斜阳只与黄昏近。

贺铸

鹧鸪天

重过阊门万事非，同来何事不同归？
梧桐半死清霜后，头白鸳鸯失伴飞。

原上草，露初晞，旧栖新垅两依依。
空床卧听南窗雨，谁复挑灯夜补衣？

捣练子

砧面莹，杵声齐，捣就征衣泪墨题。
寄到玉关应万里，戍人犹在玉关西。

唤春愁

天与多情不自由，占风流。
云闲草远絮悠悠，唤春愁。

试作小妆窥晚镜，淡蛾羞。
夕阳独倚水边楼，认归舟。

掩萧斋

落日逢迎朱雀街，共乘青舫渡秦淮，
笑捻飞絮卷金钗。

洞户华灯归别馆，碧梧红药掩萧斋。
愿随明月入君怀。

锦缠头

旧说山阴禊事修，漫书茧纸叙清游。
吴门千载更风流。

绕郭烟花连茂苑，满船丝竹载凉州，
一标争胜锦缠头。

忆秦娥

子夜歌

三更月，中庭恰照梨花雪。
梨花雪，不胜凄断，杜鹃啼血。

王孙何许音尘绝，柔桑陌上吞声别。
吞声别，陇头流水，替人呜咽。

忆秦娥

晓朦胧，前溪百鸟啼匆匆。
啼匆匆，凌波人去，拜月楼空。

去年今日东门东，鲜妆辉映桃花红。
桃花红，吹开吹落，一任东风。

青玉案

凌波不过横塘路，但目送，芳尘去。
锦瑟华年谁与度？
月桥花院，琐窗朱户，只有春知处。

飞云冉冉蘅皋暮，彩笔新题断肠句。
试问闲愁都几许？
一川烟草，满城风絮，梅子黄时雨。

菩萨蛮

彩舟载得离愁动，无端更借樵风送。
波渺夕阳迟，销魂不自持。

良宵谁与共？赖有窗间梦。
可奈梦回时，一番新别离。

清平乐

厌厌别酒，更执纤纤手。
指似归期庭下柳，一叶西风前后。

无端不系孤舟，载将多少离愁？
又是十分明月，照人两处登楼。

采桑子

东亭南馆逢迎地，几醉红裙？
凄怨离分，四叠阳关忍泪闻。

谁怜今夜篷窗雨？何处渔村？
酒冷灯昏，不许愁人不断魂。

周邦彦

兰陵王

柳阴直，烟里丝丝弄碧。
隋堤上，曾见几番，拂水飘绵送行色！
登临望故国，谁识京华倦客？
长亭路，年去岁来，应折柔条过千尺。

闲寻旧踪迹，又酒趁哀弦，灯照离席。
梨花榆火催寒食。
愁一箭风快，半篙波暖，
回头迢递便数驿，望人在天北。

凄恻，恨堆积。渐别浦萦回，津堠岑寂，
斜阳冉冉春无极。
念月榭携手，露桥闻笛。
沉思前事，似梦里，泪暗滴。

菩萨蛮

银河宛转三千曲，浴凫飞鹭澄波绿。
何处是归舟？夕阳江上楼。

天憎梅浪发，故下封枝雪。
深院卷帘看，应怜江上寒。

玉楼春

桃溪不作从容住，秋藕绝来无续处。
当时相候赤栏桥，今日独寻黄叶路。

烟中列岫青无数，雁背夕阳红欲暮。
人如风后入江云，情似雨余粘地絮。

长相思

舟中作

好风浮，晚雨收，
林叶阴阴映舣舟，斜阳明倚楼。

黯凝眸，忆旧游，
艇子扁舟来莫愁，石城风浪秋。

鹤冲天

溧水长寿乡作

梅雨霁，暑风和，高柳乱蝉多。
小园台榭远池波，鱼戏动新荷。

薄纱厨，轻羽扇，枕冷簟凉深院。
此时情绪此时天，无事小神仙。

关河令

秋阴时晴渐向暝，变一庭凄冷。
伫听寒声，云深无雁影。

更深人去寂静，但照壁孤灯相映。
酒已都醒，如何消夜永？

陈瓘

卜算子

身如一叶舟，万事从头起。
水长船高一任伊，来往洪涛里。

潮落又潮生，今古长如此。
后夜开尊独酌时，月满人千里。

谢逸

江城子

杏花村馆酒旗风，水溶溶，扬残红。
野渡舟横，杨柳绿阴浓。
梦断江南山色远，人不见，草连空。

夕阳楼外晚烟笼，粉香融，淡眉峰。
记得年时，相见画屏中。
只有关山今夜月，千里外，素光同。

毛滂

浣溪沙

初春泛舟，时北山积雪盈尺，而水南梅林盛开

水北烟寒雪似梅，水南梅闹雪千堆。
月明南北两瑶台。

云近恰如天上坐，魂清疑向斗边来。
梅花多处载春回。

浣溪沙

泛舟还余英馆

烟柳风蒲冉冉斜，小窗不用着帘遮。
载将山影转湾沙。

略彴断时分岸色，蜻蜓立处过汀花。
此情此水共天涯。

惜分飞

泪湿阑干花着露，愁到眉峰碧聚。
此恨平分取，更无言语空相觑。

断云残雨无意绪，寂寞朝朝暮暮。
今夜山深处，断魂分付潮回去。

苏庠

如梦令

雪中作

叠峰晓埋烟雨，忽作飞花无数。
整整复斜斜，来伴南枝清苦。
日暮，日暮，何许云林烟树。

谒金门

怀故居作

何处所？门外冷云堆浦。
竹里江梅寒未吐，茅屋疏疏雨。

谁遣愁来如许？小立野塘官渡。
手种凌霄今在否？柳浪迷烟渚。

菩萨蛮

周彦达舟中作

眼中叠叠烟中树，晚云点点翻荷雨。
鸥泛渚边烟，绿蒲秋满川。

未成江海去，聊作林塘主。
客恨阔无津，风斜白叠巾。

菩萨蛮

年时记着花前醉，而今花落人憔悴。
麦浪卷晴川，杜鹃声可怜。

有书无雁寄，初夏槐风细。
家在落霞边，愁逢江月圆。

浣溪沙

妙高墨梅

日暮江空船自流，谁家院落近沧洲？
一枝闲暇出墙头。

数朵幽香和月暗，十分归意为春留。
风撩片片是闲愁。

忆君王

依依宫柳拂官墙，楼殿无人春昼长。
燕子归来依旧忙。
忆君王，月破黄昏人断肠。

卜算子

往道山道中作

客舍两三花，并脸开清晓。
一朵涓涓韵已高，一朵纤纤袅。

谁与插斜红？拥髻争春好。
此意遥知梦已传，月落前村悄。

叶梦得

浣溪沙

重阳后一日极目亭

小雨初回昨夜凉，绕篱新菊已催黄。
碧空无际卷苍茫。

千里断鸿供远目，十年芳草挂愁肠。
缓歌聊与送瑶觞。

浣溪沙

送卢僎

荷叶荷花水底天，玉壶冰酒酿新泉。
一欢聊复记他年。

我亦故山归去客，与君分手暂留连。
佳人休唱好因缘。

点绛唇

绍兴乙卯登绝顶小亭

缥缈危亭，笑谈独在千峰上。
与谁同赏，万里横烟浪？

老去情怀，犹作天涯想。
空惆怅，少年豪放，莫学衰翁样！

卜算子

八月五日夜凤凰亭纳凉

新月挂林梢，暗水鸣枯沼。
时见疏星落画檐，几点流萤小。

归意已无多，故作连环绕。
欲寄新声问采菱，水阔烟波渺。

汪藻

点绛唇

新月娟娟，夜寒江静山衔斗。
起来搔首，梅影横窗瘦。

好个霜天，闲却传杯手。
君知否？乱鸦啼后，归兴浓于酒。

曹组

点绛唇

云透斜阳，半楼红影明窗户。
暮山无数，归雁愁还去。

十里平芜，花远重重树。
故人何处？可惜春将暮。

向镐

如梦令

野店几杯空酒，醉里两眉长皱。
已自不成眠，那更酒醒时候！
知否？知否？直是为他消瘦。

如梦令

谁伴明窗独坐？我和影子两个。
灯烬欲眠时，影也把人抛躲。
无那，无那，好个恓惶的我！

万俟咏

昭君怨

春到南楼雪尽，惊动灯期花信。
小雨一番寒，倚阑干。

莫把阑干频倚，一望几重烟水。
何处是京华？暮云遮。

诉衷情

送春

一鞭清晓喜还家，宿醉困流霞。
夜来小雨断霁，双燕舞风斜。

山不尽，水无涯，望中赊。
送春滋味，念远情怀，分付杨花。

长相思

雨

一声声，一更更，
窗外芭蕉窗里灯，此时无限情。

梦难成，恨难平，
不道愁人不喜听，空阶滴到明。

长相思

山驿

短长亭，古今情，
楼外凉蟾一晕生，雨余秋更清。

暮云平，暮山横，
几叶秋声和雁声，行人不要听。

陈克

豆叶黄

秋千人散小庭空，麝冷灯昏愁杀侬。
独有闲阶两袖风。月胧胧，一树梨花细雨中。

朱敦儒

鹧鸪天

西都作

我是清都山水郎，天教分付与疏狂。
曾批给雨支风券，累上留云借月章。

诗万首，酒千觞，几曾著眼看侯王？
玉楼金阙慵归去，且插梅花醉洛阳。

鹧鸪天

曾为梅花醉不归，佳人挽袖乞新词。
轻红遍写鸳鸯带，浓碧争斟翡翠卮。

人已老，事皆非。花前不饮泪沾衣。
如今但欲关门睡，一任梅花作雪飞。

鹧鸪天

画舫东时洛水清，别离心绪若为情。
西风挹泪分携后，十夜长亭九梦君。

云背水，雁回汀，只应芳草见离魂。
前回共采芙蓉处，风自凄凄月自明。

朝中措

先生笻杖是生涯，挑月更担花。
把住都无憎爱，放行总是烟霞。

飘然携去，旗亭问酒，萧寺寻茶。
恰似黄鹂无定，不知飞到谁家。

一落索

一夜雨声连晓，青灯相照。
旧时情绪此时心，花不见，人空老。

可惜春光闲了，阴多晴少。
江南江北水连云，问何处，寻芳草？

一落索

惯被好花留住，蝶飞莺语。
少年场上醉乡中，容易放，春归去。

今日江南春暮，朱颜何处？
莫将愁绪比飞花，花有数，愁无数。

十二时

连云衰草，连天晚照，连山红叶。
西风正摇落，更前溪呜咽。

燕去鸿归音信绝，问黄花，又共谁折？
征人最愁处，送寒衣时节。

好事近

渔父词

摇首出红尘，醒醉更无时节。
活计绿蓑青笠，惯披霜冲雪。

晚来风定钓丝闲，上下是新月。
千里水天一色，看孤鸿明灭。

减字木兰花

无人请我，我自铺毡松下坐。
酌酒裁诗，调弄梅花作侍儿。

心欢易醉，明月飞来花下睡。
醉舞谁知？花满纱巾月满杯。

柳梢青

红分翠别，宿酒半醒，征鞍将发。
楼外残钟，帐前残烛，窗边残月。

想伊绣枕无眠，记行客如今去也。
心下难拚，眼前难觅，口头难说。

卜算子

古涧一枝梅，免被园林锁。
路远山深不怕寒，似共春相躲。

幽思有谁知？托契都难可。
独自风流独自香，明月来寻我。

卜算子

旅雁向南飞，风雨群初失。
饥渴辛勤两翅垂，独下寒汀立。

鸥鹭苦难亲，矰缴忧相逼。
云海茫茫无处归，谁听哀鸣急？

相见欢

东风吹尽江梅，橘花开。
旧日吴王宫殿，长青苔。

今古事，英雄泪，老相催。
长恨夕阳西去，晚潮回。

相见欢

金陵城上西楼，倚清秋。
万里夕阳垂地，大江流。

中原乱，簪缨散，几时收？
试倩悲风吹泪，过扬州。

浣溪沙

满目江山忆旧游，汀洲花草弄春柔。
长亭舣住木兰舟。

好梦易随流水去，芳心空逐晓云愁，
行人莫上望京楼。

周紫芝

卜算子

席上送王彦猷

江北上归舟，再见江南岸。
江北江南几度秋，梦里朱颜换。

人是岭头云，聚散天谁管？
君似孤云何处归？我似离群雁。

鹧鸪天

一点残红欲尽时，乍凉秋气满屏帏。
梧桐叶上三更雨，叶叶声声是别离。

调宝瑟，拨金猊，那时同唱鹧鸪词。
如今风雨西楼夜，不听清歌也泪垂。

菩萨蛮

风头不定云来去，天教月到湖心住。
遥夜一襟愁，水风浑似秋。

藕花迎露笑，暗水飞萤照。
渔笛莫频吹，客愁人不知。

踏莎行

情似游丝，人如飞絮，泪珠阁定空相觑。
一溪烟柳万丝垂，无因系得兰舟住。

雁过斜阳，草迷烟渚，如今已是愁无数。
明朝且做莫思量，如何过得今宵去！

赵佶

燕山亭

裁剪冰绡，轻叠数重，淡着胭脂匀注。
新样靓妆，艳溢香融，羞杀蕊珠宫女。
易得凋零，更多少无情风雨！
愁苦，问院落凄凉，几番春暮？

凭寄离恨重重，这双燕，何曾会人言语！
天遥地远，万水千山，知他故宫何处？
怎不思量，除梦里有时曾去。
无据，和梦也新来不做。

南歌子

袅袅秋风起，萧萧败叶声。
岳阳楼上听哀筝，楼下凄凉江月，为谁明？

雾雨沉云梦，烟波渺洞庭。
可怜无处问湘灵，只有无情江水，绕江城。

如梦令

春水湖塘深处，竹暗沙洲无路。
闲伴落花来，却信东风归去。
且住，且住，细看两山烟雨。

如梦令

不见玉人清晓，长啸一声云杪。
碧水满阑塘，竹外一枝风袅。
奇妙，奇妙，半夜山空月皎。

御街行

霜风渐紧寒侵被，听孤雁，声嘹唳，
一声声送一声悲。云淡碧天如水。
披衣起告：雁儿略住，听我些儿事。

塔儿南畔城儿里，第三个桥儿外，
濑河西岸小红楼，门外梧桐雕砌。
请教且与，低声飞过，那里有人人无寐。

李清照

南歌子

天上星河转，人间帘幕垂。
凉生枕簟泪痕滋。起解罗衣，聊问夜何其？

翠贴莲蓬小，金销藕叶稀。
旧时天气旧时衣。只有情怀，不似旧家时。

如梦令

昨夜雨疏风骤，浓睡不消残酒。
试问卷帘人，却道海棠依旧。
知否？知否？应是绿肥红瘦。

凤凰台上忆吹箫

香冷金猊，被翻红浪，起来慵自梳头。
任宝奁尘满，日上帘钩。
生怕离怀别恨，多少事，欲说还休。
新来瘦，非干病酒，不是悲秋。

休休！这回去也，千万遍阳关，也则难留。
念武陵人远，烟锁秦楼。
唯有楼前流水，应念我终日凝眸。
凝眸处，从今又添，一段新愁。

一剪梅

红藕香残玉簟秋，轻解罗裳，独上兰舟。
云中谁寄锦书来？雁字回时，月满西楼。

花自飘零水自流，一种相思，两处闲愁。
此情无计可消除，才下眉头，却上心头。

醉花阴

薄雾浓云愁永昼，瑞脑销金兽。
佳节又重阳，玉枕纱橱，半夜凉初透。

东篱把酒黄昏后，有暗香盈袖。
莫道不销魂，帘卷西风。人比黄花瘦。

添字采桑子

芭蕉

窗前谁种芭蕉树？阴满中庭。
阴满中庭，叶叶心心，舒卷有余情。

伤心枕上三更雨，点滴霖霪。
点滴霖霪，愁损北人，不惯起来听。

忆秦娥

临高阁，乱山平野烟光薄。
烟光薄，栖鸦归后，暮天闻角。

断香残酒情怀恶，西风催衬梧桐落。
梧桐落，又还秋色，又还寂寞。

武陵春

风住尘香花已尽，日晚倦梳头。
物是人非事事休，欲语泪先流。

闻说双溪春尚好，也拟泛轻舟。
只恐双溪蚱蜢舟，载不动许多愁。

声声慢

寻寻觅觅，冷冷清清，凄凄惨惨戚戚。
乍暖还寒时候，最难将息。
三杯两盏淡酒，怎敌他晚来风急？
雁过也，正伤心，却是旧时相识。

满地黄花堆积，憔悴损，而今有谁堪摘！
守着窗儿，独自怎生得黑？
梧桐更兼细雨，到黄昏点点滴滴。
这次第，怎一个愁字了得！

点绛唇

寂寞深闺，柔肠一寸愁千缕。

惜春春去，几点催花雨。

倚遍阑干，只是无情绪。

人何处？连天芳草，望断归来路。

吕本中

采桑子

恨君不似江楼月，南北东西。

南北东西，只有相随无别离。

恨君却似江楼月，暂满还亏。

暂满还亏，待得团圆是几时？

减字木兰花

去年今夜，同醉月明花树下。

此夜江边，月暗长堤柳暗船。

故人何处？带我离愁江外去。

来岁花前，又是今年惜昔年。

向子諲

阮郎归

绍兴乙卯大雪行鄱阳道中

江南江北雪漫漫，遥知易水寒。
彤云深处望三关，断肠山又山。

天可老，海能翻，消除此恨难。
频闻遣使问平安，几时銮辂还？

秦楼月

芳菲歇，故园目断伤心切。
伤心切，无边烟水，无穷山色。

可堪更近乾龙节，眼中泪尽空啼血。
空啼血，子规声外，晓风残月。

生查子

近似月当怀，远似花藏雾。
好花月明时，同醉花深处。

看花不自持，对月空相顾。
愿学月频圆，莫作花飞去。

谒金门

溪声咽，溪上有人离别。
别语叮咛和泪说。罗巾沾泪血。

尽做刚肠如铁，到此也应愁绝。
回首断山帆影灭，画船空载月。

卜算子

昨夜月圆时，月下相携手。
今夜天边月又圆，夜色如清昼。

风月浑依旧，水馆空回首。
明夜归来试问伊，曾解思量否？

长相思

村姑儿，红袖衣，
初发黄梅插稻时，双双女伴随。

长歌诗，短歌诗，
歌里真情恨别离，休言伊不知。

西楼子

楼前流水悠悠，驻行舟。
满目寒云衰草，使人愁。

多少恨，多少泪，谩迟留。
何似蓦然拚舍，去来休！

如晦

卜算子

送春

有意送春归，无计留春住。
毕竟年年用著来，何似休归去！

目断楚天遥，不见春归路。
风急桃花也似愁，点点飞红雨。

王灼

点绛唇

赋登楼

休惜余春，试来把酒留春住。
问春无语，帘卷西山雨，

一掬愁心，强欲登高赋。
山无数，烟波无数，不放春归去。

长相思

来匆匆，去匆匆，
短梦无凭春又空，难随郎马踪。

山重重，水重重，
飞絮流云西复东，音书何处通？

李重元

忆王孙

春词

萋萋芳草忆王孙，柳外高楼空断魂。
杜宇声声不忍闻。
欲黄昏，雨打梨花深闭门。

聂胜琼

鹧鸪天

寄李之问

玉惨花愁出凤城，莲花楼下柳青青。
尊前一唱阳关后，别个人人第五程。

寻好梦，梦难成，况谁知我此时情？
枕前泪共帘前雨，隔个窗儿滴到明。

李弥逊

菩萨蛮

江城烽火连三月，不堪对酒长亭别。
休作断肠声，老来无泪倾。

风高帆影疾，目送舟痕碧。
锦书几时来？薰风无雁回。

陈与义

忆秦娥

五日移舟明山下作

鱼龙舞，湘君欲下潇湘浦。
潇湘浦，兴亡离合，乱波平楚。

独无尊酒酬端午，移舟来听明山雨。
明山雨，白头孤客，洞庭怀古。

浣溪沙

送了栖鸦复暮钟，栏杆生影曲屏东。
卧看孤鹤驾天风。

起舞一尊明月下，秋空如水酒如空。
谪仙已去与谁同？

点绛唇

清夜沉沉，暗蛩啼处槛花明。
乍凉帘幕，香绕屏山角。

堪恨归鸿，情似秋云薄。
书难托，尽交寂寞，忘了前时约。

菩萨蛮

春来春去催人老，老大争肯输年少？
醉后少年狂，白髭殊未妨。

插花还起舞，管领风光处。
把酒共留春，莫教花笑人！

好事近

飞雪过江来，船在赤栏桥侧。
惹报布帆无恙，着两行亲札。

从今日日在南楼，鬓自此时白。
一咏一觞谁共？负平生书册。

邓肃

长相思令

一重山，两重山，
山远天高烟水寒。相思枫叶丹。

菊花开，菊花残，
雁已西飞人未还，一帘风月闲。

长相思令

红花飞，白花飞，
郎与春风同别离，春归郎不归。

雨霏霏，雪霏霏，
又是黄昏独掩扉，孤灯隔翠帏。

岳飞

满江红

怒发冲冠，凭栏处，潇潇雨歇。
抬望眼，仰天长啸，壮怀激烈。
三十功名尘与土，八千里路云和月。
莫等闲白了少年头，空悲切！

靖康耻，犹未雪；臣子恨，何时灭？
驾长车踏破贺兰山缺。
壮志饥餐胡虏肉，笑谈渴饮匈奴血。
待从头收拾旧山河，朝天阙。

临江仙

烟柳疏疏人悄悄，画楼风外吹笙。
倚阑低唤小红声，熏香临欲睡，玉漏已三更。

坐待不来来又去，一方明月中庭。
粉墙东畔小桥横，起来花影下，扇子扑流萤。

诉衷情令

长安怀古

阿房废址汉荒丘，狐兔又群游。
豪华尽成春梦，留下古今愁。

君莫上古原头，泪难收。
夕阳西下，塞雁南飞，渭水东流。

长相思

游西湖

南高峰，北高峰，
一月湖光烟霭中。春来愁杀侬。

郎意浓，妾意浓，
油壁车轻郎马骢，相逢九里松。

卜算子

潮生浦口云，潮落津头树。
潮本无心落又生，人自来还去。

今古短长亭，送往迎来处。
老尽东西南北人，亭下潮如故。

王炎

南柯子

山冥云阴重，天寒雨意浓。
数枝幽艳湿啼红。
莫为惜花惆怅，对东风。

蓑笠朝朝出，沟塍处处通。
人间辛苦是三农。
要得一犁水足，望年丰。

韩元吉

霜天晓角

题采石蛾眉亭

倚天绝壁，直下江千尺。
天际两蛾凝黛，
愁与恨，几时极？

怒潮风正急，酒醒闻塞笛。
试问谪仙何处？
青山外，远烟碧。

好事近

汴京赐宴，闻教坊乐有感

凝碧旧池头，一听管弦凄切。
多少梨园声在，总不堪华发。

杏花无处避春愁，也傍野烟发。
唯有御沟声断，似知人呜咽。

朱淑真

清平乐

夏日游湖

恼烟撩露，留我须臾住。
携手藕花湖上路，一霎黄梅细雨。

娇痴不怕人猜，和衣睡倒人怀。
最是分携时候，归来懒傍妆台。

谒金门

春半

春已半，触目此情无限。
十二阑干闲倚遍，愁来天不管。

好是风和日暖，输与莺莺燕燕。
满院落花帘不卷，断肠芳草远。

眼儿媚

迟迟春日弄轻柔，花径暗香流。
清明过了，不堪回首，云锁珠楼。

午窗睡起莺声巧，何处唤春愁？
绿杨影里，海棠亭畔，红杏梢头。

蝶恋花

送春

楼外垂杨千万缕，欲系青春，少住春还去。
犹自风前飘柳絮，随春且看归何处？

绿满山川闻杜宇，便作无情，莫也愁人苦。
把酒问春春不语，黄昏却下潇潇雨。

减字木兰花

春怨

独行独坐，独唱独酬还独卧。
伫立伤神，无奈春寒著摸人。

此情谁见？泪洗残妆无一半。
愁病相仍，剔尽寒灯梦不成。

赵彦端

朝中措

乘风亭初成

长松擎月与天通，霜叶乱惊鸿。
露桐乍疑杯滟，云生似觉衣重。

江南胜处，青环楚嶂，红半溪枫。
倦客会应归去，一亭长枕寒空。

点绛唇

途中逢管通判

憔悴天涯，故人相逢情如故。
别离何遽？忍唱阳关句？

我是行人，更送行人去。
愁无据，寒蝉鸣处，回首斜阳暮。

卜算子

新月曲如眉，未有团圆意。
红豆不堪看，满眼相思泪。

终日擘桃穰，人在心儿里。
两朵隔墙花，早晚成连理。

姚宽

生查子

惜景

郎如陌上尘，妾似堤边絮。
相见两悠扬，踪迹无寻处。

酒面扑春风，泪眼零秋雨。
过了别离时，还解相思否？

浪淘沙

丹阳浮玉亭席上作

绿树暗长亭，几把离尊。
阳关常恨不堪闻，
何况今朝秋色里，身是行人。

清泪挹罗巾，各自销魂。
一江离恨恰平分。
安得千寻横铁锁，截断烟津？

好事近

登梅仙山绝顶望海

挥袖上西峰，孤绝去天无尺。
拄杖下临鲸海，数烟帆历历。

贪看云气舞青鸾，归路已将夕。
多谢半山松吹，解殷勤留客。

鹧鸪天

家住苍烟落照间，丝毫尘事不相关。
斟残玉瀣行穿竹，卷罢黄庭卧看山。

贪啸傲，任衰残，不妨随处一开颜，
元知造物心肠别，老却英雄似等闲。

朝中措

梅

幽姿不入少年场，无语只凄凉。
一个飘零身世，十分冷淡心肠。

江头月底，新诗旧梦，孤恨清香。
任是春风不管，也曾先识东皇。

钗头凤

红酥手，黄藤酒，满城春色官墙柳。
东风恶，欢情薄。一怀愁绪，几年离索。
错，错，错！

春如旧，人空瘦，泪痕红浥鲛绡透。
桃花落，闲池阁。山盟虽在，锦书难托。
莫，莫，莫！

长相思

面苍然，鬓蟠然，
满腹诗书不值钱。官闲常昼眠。

画凌烟，上甘泉，
自古功名属少年。知心惟杜鹃。

诉衷情

当年万里觅封侯，匹马戍凉州。
关河梦断何处？尘暗旧貂裘。

胡未灭，鬓先秋，泪空流。
此生谁料？心在天山，身老沧洲！

唐婉

钗头凤

世情薄，人情恶，雨送黄昏花易落。
晓风干，泪痕残。欲笺心事，独语斜阑。
难，难，难！

人成各，今非昨，病魂常似秋千索。
角声寒，夜阑珊。怕人寻问，咽泪装欢。
瞒，瞒，瞒！

范成大

南柯子

怅望梅花驿，凝情杜若洲。
香云低处有高楼，可惜高楼，不近木兰舟。

缄素双鱼远，题红片叶秋。
欲凭江水寄离愁，江水东流，那肯更西流？

秦楼月

楼阴缺，阑干影卧东厢月。
东厢月，一天风露，杏花如雪。

隔烟催漏金虬咽，罗帏暗淡灯花结。
灯花结，片时春梦，江南天阔。

游次公

卜算子

风雨送人来，风雨留人住。
草草杯盘话别离，风雨催人去。

泪眼不曾晴，眉黛愁还聚。
明日相思莫上楼，楼上多风雨。

杨万里

好事近

七月十三日夜登万花川谷望月作

月未到诚斋，先到万花川谷。
不是诚斋无月，隔一林修竹。

如今才是十三夜，月色已如玉。
未是秋光奇绝，看十五十六。

如梦令

道是梨花不是，道是杏花不是。

白白与红红，别是东风情味。

曾记，曾记，人在武陵微醉。

卜算子

不是爱风尘，似被前缘误。

花落花开自有时，总赖东君主。

去也终须去，住也如何住？

若得山花插满头，莫问奴归处。

浣溪沙

霜日明霄水蘸空，鸣鞘声里绣旗红。

淡烟衰草有无中。

万里中原烽火北，一尊浊酒戍楼东。

酒阑挥泪向悲风。

西江月

阻风三峰下

满载一船秋色，平铺十里湖光。
波神留我看斜阳，放起鳞鳞细浪。

明日风回更好，今宵露宿何妨？
水晶官里奏霓裳，准拟岳阳楼上。

卜算子

风生杜若洲，日暮垂杨浦。
行到田田乱叶边，不见凌波女。

独自倚危栏，欲向荷花语。
无奈荷花不应人，背立啼红雨。

辛弃疾

摸鱼儿

更能消几番风雨？匆匆春又归去。
惜春长怕花开早，何况落红无数！
春且住！见说道，天涯芳草无归路。
怨春不语。算只有殷勤画檐蛛网，尽日惹飞絮。

长门事，准拟佳期又误。蛾眉曾有人妒。
千金纵买相如赋，默默此情谁诉？
君莫舞！君不见，玉环飞燕皆尘土？
闲愁最苦。休去倚危栏！斜阳正在烟柳断肠处。

菩萨蛮

书江西造口壁

郁孤台下清江水，中间多少行人泪。
西北望长安，可怜无数山。

青山遮不住，毕竟东流去。
江晚正愁予，山深闻鹧鸪。

祝英台近

晚春

宝钗分，桃叶渡，烟柳暗南浦。
怕上层楼，十日九风雨。
断肠片片飞红，都无人管，更谁劝啼莺声住？

鬓边觑，试把花卜归期，才簪又重数。
罗帐灯昏，哽咽梦中语：
是他春带愁来，春归何处？却不解带将愁去！

清平乐

茅檐低小，溪上青青草。
醉里吴音相媚好，白发谁家翁媪？

大儿锄豆溪东，中儿正织鸡笼。
最喜小儿无赖，溪头卧剥莲蓬。

清平乐

独宿博山王氏庵

绕床饥鼠，蝙蝠翻灯舞。
屋上松风吹急雨，破纸窗前自语。

平生塞北江南，归来华发苍颜。
布被秋宵梦觉，眼前万里江山。

西江月

夜行黄沙道中

明月别枝惊鹊，清风半夜鸣蝉。
稻花香里说丰年，听取蛙声一片。

七八个星天外，两三点雨山前。
旧时茅店社林边，路转溪桥忽现。

西江月

遣兴

醉里且贪欢笑，要愁那得功夫？
近来始觉古人书，信着全无是处。

昨夜松边醉倒，问松我醉何如？
只疑松动要来扶，以手推松曰去！

贺新郎

甚矣吾衰矣，怅平生，交游零落，只今余几！
白发空垂三千丈，一笑人间万事。
问何物能令公喜？
我见青山多妩媚，料青山见我应如是。
情与貌，略相似。

一尊搔首东窗里，想渊明《停云》诗就，此时风味。
江左沉酣求名者，岂识浊醪妙理？
回首叫云飞风起。
不恨古人吾不见，恨古人不见吾狂耳。
知我者，二三子。

丑奴儿

书博山道中壁

少年不识愁滋味，爱上层楼。
爱上层楼，为赋新词强说愁。

而今识尽愁滋味，欲说还休。
欲说还休，却道天凉好个秋。

鹧鸪天

壮岁旌旗拥万夫，锦襜突骑渡江初。
燕兵夜娖银胡䩮，汉箭朝飞金仆姑。

追往事，叹今吾，春风不染白髭须。
却将万字平戎策，换得东家种树书。

卜算子

刚者不坚牢，柔底难摧挫。
不信张开口角看，舌在牙先堕。

已阙两边厢，又豁中间个。
说与儿曹莫笑翁，狗窦从君过。

水龙吟

登建康赏心亭

楚天千里清秋，水随天去秋无际。
遥岑远目，献愁供恨，玉簪螺髻。
落日楼头，断鸿声里，江南游子，
把吴钩看了，栏杆拍遍，无人会，登临意。

休说鲈鱼堪脍，尽西风，季鹰归未？
求田问舍，怕应羞见，刘郎才气。
可惜流年，忧愁风雨，树犹如此。
倩何人唤取，红巾翠袖，揾英雄泪？

武陵春

走去走来三百里，五日以为期。
六日归来已是疑，应是望多时。

鞭个马儿归去也，心急马行迟。
不免相烦喜鹊儿，先报那人知。

最高楼

吾衰矣！须富贵何时？富贵是危机。
暂忘设醴抽身去，未曾得米弃官归。
穆先生，陶县令，是吾师。

待葺个园儿名佚老，更作个亭儿名亦好。
闲饮酒，醉吟诗。
千年田换八百主，一人口插几张匙？
便休休！更说甚，是和非？

陈亮

好事近

咏梅

的烁两三枝，点破暮烟苍碧，
好在屋檐斜入，傍玉奴吹笛。

月华如水过林塘，花阴弄苔石。
欲向梦中飞蝶，恐幽香难觅。

虞美人

春愁

东风荡飏轻云缕，时送潇潇雨。
水边台榭燕新归，一口香泥，湿带落花飞。

海棠糁径铺香绣，依旧成春瘦。
黄昏庭院柳啼鸦，记得那人，和月折梨花。

刘过

沁园春

寄辛承旨。时承旨招，不赴

斗酒彘肩，风雨渡江，岂不快哉！
被香山居士，约林和靖，与坡仙老，驾勒吾回。
坡谓："西湖正如西子，浓抹淡妆临镜台。"
二公者，皆掉头不顾，只管衔杯。

白云："天竺去来，图画里，峥嵘楼观开。
爱东西双涧，纵横水绕；两峰南北，高下云堆。"
逋曰："不然。暗香浮动，争似孤山先探梅。
须晴去，访稼轩未晚。且此徘徊。"

天仙子

初赴省别妾于三十里头

别酒醺醺浑易醉，回过头来三十里。
马儿不住去如飞，
牵一憩，坐一憩，断送煞人山与水。

是则是功名终可喜，不道恩情拚得未！
云迷村店酒旗斜。
去也是，住也是，烦恼自家烦恼你。

行香子

同郭季端访旧不遇有作

一琐窗儿明快，料想那人不在。
熏笼脱下旧衣裳，件件香难赛。

匆匆去得忒煞，这镜儿也不曾盖。
千朝百日不曾来，没这些儿个采！

醉太平

情高意真，眉长鬓青。
小楼明月调筝，写春风数声。

思君忆君，魂牵梦萦。
翠绡香暖熏云屏，更那堪酒醒！

糖多令

重过武昌

芦叶满汀洲，寒沙带浅流。二十年重过南楼。
柳下系舟犹未稳，能几日，又中秋？

黄鹤断矶头，故人曾到否？旧江山浑是新愁。
欲买桂花同载酒，终不似，少年游。

姜夔

点绛唇

丁未冬过吴松作

燕雁无心，太湖西畔随云去。
数峰清苦，商略黄昏雨。

第四桥边，拟共天随住。
今何许？凭阑怀古，残柳参差舞。

忆王孙

鄱阳彭氏小楼作

冷红叶叶下塘秋，长与行云共一舟。
零落江南不自由。
两绸缪，料得吟鸾夜夜愁。

鹧鸪天

元夜有所梦

肥水东流无尽期，当初不合种相思。
梦中未比丹青见，暗里忽惊山鸟啼。

春未绿，鬓先丝，人间别久不成悲。
谁教岁岁红莲夜，两处沉吟各自知。

踏莎行

江上感梦而作

燕燕轻盈，莺莺娇软，分明又向华胥见。
夜长争得薄情知？春初早被相思染。

别后书辞，别时针线，离魂暗逐郎行远。
淮南皓月冷千山，冥冥归去无人管。

浣溪沙

著酒行行满袂风，草枯霜鹘落晴空。
销魂都在夕阳中。

恨入四弦人欲老，梦寻千驿意难通。
当时何似莫匆匆！

扬州慢

淮左名都，竹西佳处，解鞍少驻初程。
过春风十里，尽荠麦青青。
自胡马窥江去后，废池乔木，犹厌言兵。
渐黄昏，清角吹寒，都在空城。

杜郎俊赏，算而今重到须惊。
纵豆蔻词工，青楼梦好，难赋深情。
二十四桥仍在，波心荡，冷月无声。
念桥边红药，年年知为谁生！

史达祖

双双燕

过春社了，度帘幕中间，去年尘冷。
差池欲住，时入旧巢相并。
还相雕梁藻井，又软语商量不定。
飘然快拂花梢，翠尾分开红影。

芳径，芹泥雨润，爱贴地争飞，竞夸轻俊。
红楼归晚，看足柳昏花暝。
应自栖香正稳，便忘了天涯芳信。
愁损翠黛双蛾，日日画阑独凭。

阮郎归

月下感事

旧时明月旧时身，旧时梅萼新。
旧时月底似梅人，梅春人不春。

香入梦，粉成尘，情多多断魂。
芙蓉孔雀夜温温，愁痕即泪痕。

临江仙

草脚青回细腻，柳梢绿转苗条。
旧游重到合魂销。
棹横青水渡，人凭赤阑桥。

归梦有诗曾见，新愁未肯相饶。
酒香红被夜迢迢。
莫教无用月，来照可怜宵！

解佩令

人行花坞，衣沾香雾，有新词逢春分付。
屡欲传情，奈燕子不曾飞去，倚珠帘咏郎秀句。

相思一度，秾愁一度，最难忘遮灯私语。
淡月梨花，借梦来花边廊庑，指春衫泪曾溅处。

黄机

忆秦娥

秋萧索，梧桐落尽西风恶。

西风恶，数声新雁，数声残角。

离愁不管人飘泊，年年孤负黄花约。

黄花约，几重庭院？几重帘幕？

张辑

月上瓜洲

南徐多景楼作

江头又见新秋，几多愁？

塞草连天，何处是神州？

英雄恨，古今泪，水东流。

唯有渔竿明月，上瓜洲。

严仁

诉衷情

章贡别怀

一声水调解兰舟，人间无此愁。

无情江水东流去，与我泪争流。

人已远，更回头，苦凝眸。

断魂何处？梅花岸曲，小小红楼。

刘克庄

沁园春

梦孚若

何处相逢？登宝钗楼，访铜雀台。

唤厨人斫就，东溟鲸脍；

围人呈罢，西极龙媒。

天下英雄，使君与操，余子谁堪共酒杯？

车千乘，载燕北赵南，剑客奇才。

饮酣画鼓如雷，谁信被晨鸡轻唤回！

叹年光过尽，功名未立，

书生老去，机会方来。

使李将军遇高皇帝，万户侯何足道哉！

披衣起，但凄凉感旧，慷慨生哀。

清平乐

五月十五夜玩月

纤云扫迹，万顷玻璃色。

醉跨玉龙游八极，历历天青海碧。

水晶宫殿飘香，群仙方按霓裳。

消得几多风露，变教人世清凉？

清平乐

五月十五夜玩月

风高浪快，万里骑蟾背。
曾识姮娥真体态，素面元无粉黛。

身游银阙珠宫，俯看积气濛濛。
醉里偶摇桂树，人间唤作凉风。

清平乐

赠陈参议师文家侍儿

宫腰束素，只怕能轻举。
好筑避风台护取，莫遣惊鸿飞去。

一团香玉温柔，笑罄俱有风流。
贪与萧郎眉语，不知舞错伊州。

卜算子

片片蝶衣轻，点点猩红小。
道是天公不惜花，百种千般巧。

朝见树头繁，暮见枝头少。
道是天公果惜花，雨洗风吹了。

吴文英

浣溪沙

门隔花深梦旧游，夕阳无语燕归愁。
玉纤香动小帘钩。

落絮无声春堕泪，行云有影月含羞。
春风临夜冷于秋。

风入松

听风听雨过清明，愁草瘗花铭。
门前绿暗分携路，一丝柳，一寸柔情。
料峭春寒中酒，交加晓梦啼莺。

西园日日扫林亭，依旧赏新晴。
黄蜂频扑秋千索，有当时纤手香凝。
惆怅双鸳不到，幽阶一夜苔生。

糖多令

何处合成愁？离人心上秋。纵芭蕉不雨也飕飕。
都道晚凉天气好，有明月，怕登楼。

年事梦中休，花空烟水流。燕辞归，客尚淹留。
垂柳不萦裙带住，漫长是系行舟。

醉桃源

赠卢长笛

沙河塘上旧游嬉，卢郎少年时。
一声长笛月中吹，和云和雁飞。

惊物换，叹星移。相看两鬓丝。
断肠吴苑草萋萋，倚楼人未归。

刘辰翁

柳梢青

铁马蒙毡，银花洒泪，春入愁城。
笛里番腔，街头戏鼓，不是歌声。

那堪独坐青灯，想故国、高台月明。
辇下风光，山中岁月，海上心情！

周密

闻鹊喜

吴山观涛

天水碧，染就一江秋色。
鳌戴雪山龙起蛰，快风吹海立。

数点烟鬟青滴，一杼霞绡红湿。
白鸟明边帆影直，隔江闻夜笛。

文天祥

酹江月

乾坤能大，算蛟龙元不是池中物。
风雨牢愁无着处，那更寒虫四壁？
横槊赋诗，登楼作赋，万事空中雪。
江流如此，方来还有英杰。

堪笑一叶漂零，重来淮水，正凉风新发。
镜里朱颜都变尽，只有丹心难灭。
去去龙沙，江山回首，一线青如发。
故人应念，杜鹃枝上残月。

王沂孙

齐天乐

蝉

一襟余恨宫魂断，年年翠阴庭树。
乍咽凉柯，还移暗叶，重把离愁深诉。
西窗过雨，怪瑶佩流空，玉筝调柱。
镜暗妆残，为谁娇鬓尚如许？

铜仙铅泪似洗，叹移盘去远，难贮零露。
病翼惊秋，枯形阅世，消得斜阳几度？
余音更苦，甚独抱清霜，顿成凄楚！
谩想薰风，柳丝千万缕。

一剪梅

舟过吴江

一片春愁待酒浇，江上舟摇，楼上帘招。
秋娘渡与泰娘桥，风又飘飘，雨又潇潇。

何日归家洗客袍？银字笙调，心字香烧。
流光容易把人抛，红了樱桃，绿了芭蕉。

虞美人

听雨

少年听雨歌楼上，红烛昏罗帐。
壮年听雨客舟中，江阔云低，断雁叫西风。

而今听雨僧庐下，鬓已星星也。
悲欢离合总无情，一任阶前，点滴到天明。

霜天晓角

人影窗纱，是谁来摘花？
折则从他折去，知折去向谁家？

檐牙，枝最佳。折时高折些。
说与折花人道：须插向，鬓边斜。

张炎

四字令

莺吟翠屏，帘吹絮云。
东风也怕花嗔，带飞花赶春。

邻娃笑迎，嬉游趁晴。
明朝何处相寻？那人家柳阴。

烛影摇红

答邵素心

隔水呼舟，采香何处追游好？
一年春事二分花，犹有花多少？

容易繁华过了，趁园林飞红未扫。
旧醒新醉，几日不来，绿杨芳草。

珍珠令

桃花扇底歌声杳。愁多少？便觉道花阴闲了。
因甚不归来？甚归来不早？

满院飞花休要扫，待留与薄情知道。
知道，怕一似飞花，和春都老！

THEORY ON LITERARY TRANSLATION OF THE CHINESE SCHOOL

The theory on literary translation of the Chinese school owes its origin to traditional Chinese culture, including the Confucian and the Taoist school of thought respectively represented by *Thus Spoke the Master* and *Laws Divine and Human*.

It is said in the first chapter of *Laws Divine and Human* that truth can be known, but it may not be the truth you know, and that things may be named, but names are not the things. When applied to literary translation, this may mean that the theory on literary translation can be known, but it may not the unproven theory on the one hand, nor the scientific theory on the other, for neither literary translation nor its theory is science. As the names are not equal to the things, the translation cannot be equal to the original. As there is more difference than equivalence between the Chinese and the English language, the principle of equivalence can not be applied to the translation between them as between two occidental languages.

It is said in the last chapter of *Laws Divine and Human* that truthful words may not be beautiful and beautiful words may not be truthful. That is to say, there is contradiction between truth and beauty or between equivalence and excellence. A translation where equivalents are used may be called a faithful or truthful translation. When no equivalent can be found between two languages, the translator should make use of the best expressions or excellent expressions of the target language. That may be called theory of excellence.

In *Thus Spoke the Master*, Confucius said, "At seventy, I can do what I will without going beyond what is right." Professor Zhu Guangqian said that this has shown the mature state of an artist. I think it may also show the mature state of a literary translator. The literal translator has used the equivalents without going beyond the original in sound; the liberal translator has described the image without going beyond the original in sense; the literary translator has described the scene without going beyond reality. Not to go beyond the original is to be truthful or faithful, and the translator has reached the ordinary level of translation. To do what one will without going beyond the original is not only to be faithful but also to make his translation beautiful, in that case the translator has attained a higher level. To excel the original without going beyond the reality it describes is to attain the highest level.

What is literary translation? It is an art of solving the contradiction between faithfulness (or truth) and beauty. How to solve it? There are three methods, namely, equalization, generalization and particularization. When there is little or no contradition between truth and beauty, equalization or equivalents may be used. When there is contradction between them, generalization may be used to make the meaning clear, and particularization to make a deeper impression.

Confucius said in *Thus Spoke the Master* that it would be good to be understandable, better to be enjoyable and best to be delectable or delightful. When applied to literary translation, this principle means that an understandable translation is good, an enjoyable one is better and a delightful one is best. The ontology or theory of contradition between truth and beauty, the methodology or theory of equalization, generalization and particularization, and the teleology or theory of the understandable, the enjoyable and the delectable, all owe their origin to the Confucian and Taoist schools of thoughts.

But Confucius said less about what delight is and more about how to be delightful. In the beginning of *Thus Spoke the Master* he said it is delightful to acquire knowledge and put it into practice; In Chapter Six he told us how Yan Hui could find delight in reading though living in a humble lane with only a handful of rice to eat and a gourdful of water to drink; In Chapter Eleven, Zeng Xi told us his delight in an spring excursion. From these examples we can see Confucius' theory on delight or teleology, and his theory on practice or methodology. His theory is not scientific but artistic. Since literary translation is an art but not a branch of science, his theory can not only be applied to the practice but also to the theory of literary translation. As his theory has stood the test of time, it is as durable as scientific theories. A theorist on science who studies truth and the truthful should not go beyond what is truthful. A theorist on art or an artist who studies beauty and the beautiful may go beyond what is truthful and faithful.

The contradiction between truth and beauty in Chinese theory on literary translation has developed into a contradiction between equivalence and excellence. As Keats said, "Beauty is truth, truth beauty," we may even say beauty is a virtue, a kind of excellence. When we cannot find the equivalent, we may resort to generalization or particularization.

In short, literary translation is an art to create the beautiful. This is the epistemology of the Chinese school. The contradition between truth and beauty or between equivalence and excellence is its ontology; the theory on equalization, generalization and particularization is its triple methodology; and the theory of the understandable, the enjoyable and the delectable or delightful is its triple teleology.

Xu Yuanchong
Oct. 2011

代后记：中国学派的文学翻译理论

　　中国学派的文学翻译理论源自中国的传统文化，主要包括儒家思想和道家思想，儒家思想的代表著作是《论语》，道家思想的代表著作是《老子道德经》。

　　《老子道德经》第一章开始就说："道可道，非常道；名可名，非常名。"联系到翻译理论上来，就是说：翻译理论是可以知道的，是可以说得出来的，但不是只说得出来而经不起实践检验的空头理论，这就是中国学派翻译理论中的实践论。其次，文学翻译理论不能算科学理论（自然科学），与其说是社会科学理论，不如说是人文学科或艺术理论，这就是文学翻译的艺术论，也可以说是相对论。后六个字"名可名，非常名"应用到文学翻译理论上来，可以有两层意思：第一层是原文的文字是描写现实的，但并不等于现实，文字和现实之间还有距离，还有矛盾；第二层意思是译文和原文之间也有距离，也有矛盾，译文和原文所描写的现实之间，自然还有距离，还有矛盾。译文应该发挥译语优势，运用最好的译语表达方式，来和原文展开竞赛，使译文和现实的距离或矛盾小于原文和现实之间的矛盾，那就是超越原文了。这就是文学翻译理论中的优势论或优化论，超越论或竞赛论。文学翻译理论应该解决的不只是译文和原文在文字方面的矛盾，还要解决译文和原文所反映的现实之间的矛盾，这是文学翻译的本体论。

　　一般翻译只要解决"真"或"信"或"似"的问题，文学翻译却要解决"真"或"信"和"美"之间的矛盾。原文反映的现实不只是言内之意，还有言外之意。中国的文学语言往往有言外之意，甚至还有言外之情。文学翻译理论也要解决译文和原文的言外之意、言外之情的矛盾。

《论语》说："知之者不如好之者，好之者不如乐之者。"知之，好之，乐之，这"三之论"是对艺术论的进一步说明。艺术论第一条原则要求译文忠实于原文所反映的现实，求的是真，可以使人知之；第二条原则要求用"三化"法来优化译文，求的是美，可以使人好之；第三条原则要求用"三美"来优化译文，尤其是译诗词，求的是意美、音美和形美，可以使人乐之。如果"不逾矩"的等化译文能使人知之（理解），那就达到了文学翻译的低标准，如从心所欲而不逾矩的浅化或深化的译文既能使人知之，又能使人好之（喜欢），那就达到了中标准；如果从心所欲的译文不但能使人知之，好之，还能使人乐之（愉快），那才达到了文学翻译的高标准。这也是中国译者对世界译论作出的贡献。

翻译艺术的规律是从心所欲而不逾矩。"矩"就是规矩，规律。但艺术规律却可以依人的主观意志而转移，是因为得到承认才算正确的。所以贝多芬说：为了更美，没有什么清规戒律不可打破。他所说的戒律不是科学规律，而是艺术规律。不能用科学规律来评论文学翻译。

孔子不大谈"什么是"（What?）而多谈"怎么做"（How?）。这是中国传统的方法论，比西方流传更久，影响更广，作用更大，并且经过了两三千年实践的考验。《论语》第一章中说："学而时习之，不亦说（悦，乐）乎！""学"是取得知识，"习"是实践。孔子只说学习实践可以得到乐趣，却不说什么是"乐"。这就是孔子的方法论，是中国文学翻译理论的依据。

总而言之，中国学派的文学翻译理论是研究老子提出的

"信"（似）"美"（优）矛盾的艺术（本体论），但"信"不限原文，还指原文所反映的现实，这是认识论，"信"由严复提出的"信达雅"发展到鲁迅提出"信顺"的直译，再发展到陈源的"三似"（形似，意似，神似），直到傅雷的"重神似不重形似"，这已经接近"美"了。"美"发展到鲁迅的"三美"（意美，音美，形美），再发展到林语堂提出的"忠实，通顺，美"，转化为朱生豪"传达原作意趣"的意译，直到茅盾提出的"美的享受"。孔子提出的"从心所欲"发展到郭沫若提出的创译论（好的翻译等于创作），以及钱钟书说的译文可以胜过原作的"化境"说，再发展到优化论，超越论，"三化"（等化，浅化，深化）方法论。孔子提出的"不逾矩"和老子说的"信言不美，美言不信"有同有异。老子"信美"并重，孔子"从心所欲"重于"不逾矩"，发展为朱光潜的"艺术论"，包括郭沫若说的"在信达之外，愈雅愈好。所谓'雅'不是高深或讲修饰，而是文学价值或艺术价值比较高。"直到茅盾说的："必须把文学翻译工作提高到艺术创造的水平。"孔子的"乐之"发展为胡适之的"愉快"说（翻译要使读者读得愉快），再发展到"三之"（知之，好之，乐之）目的论。这就是中国学派的文学翻译理论发展为"美化之艺术"（"三美"，"三化"，"三之"的艺术）的概况。

许渊冲
2011年10月

图书在版编目（CIP）数据

宋词三百首: 汉英对照 / 许渊冲译. — 北京: 五洲传播出版社,
2018.1 (2021.8重印)

（许译中国经典诗文集）

ISBN 978-7-5085-3897-6

Ⅰ.①宋… Ⅱ.①许… Ⅲ.①宋词－选集－汉、英 Ⅳ.①H319.4：I

中国版本图书馆CIP数据核字(2017)第323691号

宋词三百首

译　　者：	许渊冲
策划编辑：	荆孝敏　郑　磊
责任编辑：	王　峰
中文编辑：	孟学文
英文编辑：	马培武　郁　辉
装帧设计：	北京正视文化艺术有限责任公司
出版发行：	五洲传播出版社
地　　址：	北京市海淀区北三环中路31号生产力大楼B座6层
邮　　编：	100088
电　　话：	010-82005927，010-82007837
网　　址：	http://www.cicc.org.cn　http://www.thatsbooks.com
印　　刷：	北京市房山腾龙印刷厂
版　　次：	2012年1月第1版　2021年8月第2版第4次印刷
开　　本：	140mm×210mm　1/32
印　　张：	11.75
字　　数：	300千字
书　　号：	ISBN 978-7-5085-3897-6
定　　价：	89.00元